FINALS
Property

CORE CONCEPTS AND KEY QUESTIONS

Robert Feinberg, Esq.
Editorial Consultant

PUBLISHING

New York

This publication is designed to provide accurate and authoritative information in regard to the subject matter covered. It is sold with the understanding that the publisher is not engaged in rendering legal, accounting, or other professional service. If legal advice or other expert assistance is required, the services of a competent professional should be sought.

Series Editor: Lisa T. McElroy, Associate Professor, Drexel University College of Law
Editorial Director: Jennifer Farthing
Editor: Michael Sprague
Production Editor: Fred Urfer
Cover Designer: Carly Schnur

Published by Kaplan Publishing, a division of Kaplan, Inc.
1 Liberty Plaza, 24th floor
New York, NY 10006

Printed in the United States of America

August 2007
10   9   8   7   6   5   4   3   2

ISBN13: 978-1-4277-9642-4

Kaplan Publishing books are available at special quantity discounts to use for sales promotions, employee premiums, or educational purposes. Please email our Special Sales Department to order or for more information at kaplanpublishing@kaplan.com, or write to Kaplan Publishing, 1 Liberty Plaza, 24th floor, New York, NY 10006.

(3) Junior interests
(4) Purchase money mortgages
7. Deficiency Judgments
   a. Limitations
8. Installment Land Sale Contracts
   a. Default
      (1) Forfeiture
      (2) Grace period
      (3) Forfeiture and restitution
      (4) Foreclosure
      (5) Waiver of strict performance

Kaplan PMBR Finals: Core Concepts and Key Questions is a law school preparatory series from one of the leading companies for preparing for the Bar exam. It is designed to provide students with focused study to succeed on their law school exams. Remember that *Kaplan PMBR* is not simply another commercial outline series. Rather each edition consists of several integrated sections. This edition contains a substantive outline, capsule summary outlines, objective law school exam questions, essay exam questions, and fully detailed explanatory answers.

Finals is designed to be used as a pre-exam study aid. You should be aware that most law schools are now implementing objective and essay questions on their final examinations. In the past virtually all law school exams were written solely in an essay format. Now the trend is to test students with objective and subjective questions.

Objective questions on exams eliminate the subjectivity of essay grading. They provide uniformity and a basis for reliable grading. Law schools are also recognizing the necessity to prepare students for the Multistate Bar Examination (commonly referred to as the "MBE"). The MBE is a uniform, national, 200-question multiple choice exam covering the six subject areas of Torts, Contracts, Real Property/Future Interests, Evidence, Constitutional Law, and Criminal Law/Procedure.

Finals is designed as a national law school study aid. Many of the questions and answers follow the majority rule of law in effect in most jurisdictions. Many of the rationales and explanations refer to the national norm. This is to make the series as applicable as possible for students across the country.

This edition includes 100 multiple choice questions to review Property. The questions require knowledge of the black letter law and some legal reasoning skills. Reviewing the questions will help you prepare for your exams and assist you in your comfort with the black letter law.

Kaplan and PMBR wish you the best of luck on your exams and in your legal career.

I. ESTATES IN LAND

A. PRESENT POSSESSORY ESTATES

1. In General

An estate in land is an interest that is or may become possessory. Land may be subject to ownership by two or more persons holding separate and distinct estates. At any given time, only one possessory estate may exist. Interests which may become possessory at some future time are called future interests. Freehold estates give possession through legal title or a right to hold. Nonfreehold estates give mere possession.

2. Fee Simple Absolute

A fee simple (absolute) is the most extensive estate with a potentially infinite duration. "Fee" indicates an estate of inheritance. "Simple" signifies that there are no restrictions on the estate with respect to inheritance.

Example: O to A and his heirs (at common law), or
O to A (at modern law).

O | A's fee simple (absolute) ⟶

a. At common law, words of inheritance were required to designate the estate transferred (*i.e.,* "and his heirs" for a fee simple conveyance to a human being and "successors" for a fee simple transfer to a corporation). Words of inheritance were not required for a conveyance by will, a conveyance to a trustee, or a partition between concurrent owners except in the case of tenants in common.

b. Usually words such as "heirs" and "heirs of the body" are considered words of limitation designating the fact that the grantee acquires an estate in fee.

c. Words of purchase are words used to indicate an intention to convey an estate to a specific person.

3. Fee Simple Determinable (and Possibility of Reverter)

A fee simple determinable is a fee simple estate created to continue *until some specified event occurs. The estate terminates automatically.* Practically all American states recognize the fee simple determinable.

Example: O to A so long as the property is used as a school.

O | A's fee simple determinable ⟶

O's possibility of reverter ⟶

a. **Distinguished from Fee Simple Subject to Condition Subsequent**

The principal difference between the two is this: in the determinable fee the estate *automatically* comes to an end when the stated event happens, whereas in the fee simple subject to condition subsequent the termination of the estate is *not automatic* but must be terminated by the entry or exercise of the reserved power by the grantor (or his successor in interest).

b. **Creation of Fee Simple Determinable**

The typical words for creating a determinable fee are:

(1) "so long as,"

(2) "during,"

(3) "until,"

(4) "while."

Note: When none of these expressions is used, the key factor is the *intent of the grantor* as expressed in the conveyance (namely, did the grantor intend for title to automatically revert back or did he want to take affirmative steps to get title back?).

c. **Possibility of Reverter**

Since the grantee's estate may end (upon the happening or non-happening of a stated event) there is a possibility that the land may *revert back* to the grantor. Thus, the interest which is left in a grantor (who conveys an estate in fee simple determinable) is called a "possibility of reverter."

4. **Fee Simple Subject to a Condition Subsequent**

A fee simple subject to a condition subsequent is a fee simple estate that may be terminated upon the happening of a named event by the grantor or his successors in interest. The estate continues until the grantor or the future interest holder exercises his right of entry or power of termination. The majority of American states recognize this type of estate.

Example: O to A and his heirs, but if the land is not used as a farm, O may reenter the land.

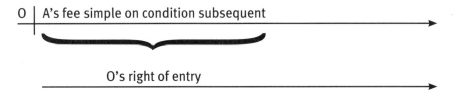

O | A's fee simple on condition subsequent

O's right of entry

a. **Mode of Creating**

A fee simple on condition subsequent is generally introduced by such phrases as:

(1) "on condition that,"

(2) "subject to the condition that,"

(3) "but if."

Note: An express reverter clause giving the grantor the right of reentry is generally appended. However, a reentry clause is not essential to create this estate. Extrinsic evidence is admissible to resolve ambiguity to determine the true intention of the grantor when a reentry clause is not present.

b. **Right of Entry**

In general, a right of entry (or reentry) can be created only in favor of the grantor or his heirs. If created in favor of a third party, the interest is called an executory interest (e.g., "if the property is ever used for other than residential purposes, then to C and his heirs"). Unlike a right of entry, an executory limitation is subject to the Rule Against Perpetuities.

MULTISTATE NUANCE CHART:

FEE SIMPLE DETERMINABLE	FEE SIMPLE SUBJECT TO CONDITION SUBSEQUENT
1. Possibility of reverter (which means the fee simple estate is subject to a special limitation).	1. Right of reentry (which means the fee simple estate is subject to being terminated by the *reentry of the grantor*).
2. Estate terminates *automatically by operation of law* upon the happening (or non-happening) of a stated event or condition.	2. Estate will continue in the grantee (or his successors) unless and until the grantor exercises his power of termination.
3. Legal effect: automatic reversion to the grantor (or those claiming under him) when the event occurs.	3. Grantor's reentry effectuates a termination of grantee's estate.
4. Usually created by the words "until" or "so long as."	4. Estate does not end, *ipso facto*, upon the happening of the stated event, but rather upon grantor's exercising his right of reentry.
	5. Usually created by such words as "upon condition that," "provided that," or "but if" and coupled with a provision for reentry.

5. **Fee Simple Subject to Executory Interest**

A fee simple subject to executory interest is a fee simple estate, whereupon the happening of a named event, ownership is to pass from the grantee to one other than the grantor. The future interest created in the third party is an executory interest.

   a. **A *shifting executory interest*** is one where the right to possession shifts from one grantee to another grantee.

Example: O to A and his heirs as long as the land is farmed, then to B and his heirs.

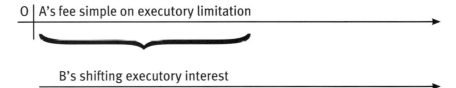

   O | A's fee simple on executory limitation

   B's shifting executory interest

Example: O to A and his heirs, but if B returns from Brazil, then to B and his heirs.

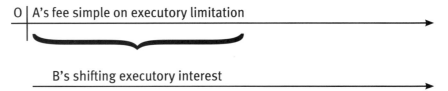

   O | A's fee simple on executory limitation

   B's shifting executory interest

   b. **A *springing executory interest*** is one where the right to possession springs from the grantor to the grantee.

Example: O to A for life, and one year later, to B and his heirs.

O	A's life estate	O's reversion in	B's springing
		fee simple on executory limitation	executory interest

Example: O to A and his heirs upon A's marriage.

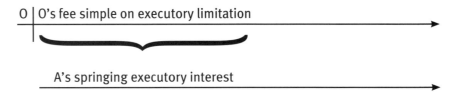

   O | O's fee simple on executory limitation

   A's springing executory interest

6. **Fee Tail**

At common law, a fee tail was usually created by the words, "to B and the heirs of his body." Inheritance was restricted to lineal descendants of the grantee.

   a. Inheritance could be ***restricted to a particular group of lineal descendants*** of the grantee by proper words of limitation.

(1) A grant to a male and the male heirs of his body created a fee tail male.

(2) A grant to a female and the female heirs of her body created a fee tail female.

(3) A grant to a donee and the heirs of his or her body by a particular spouse created a fee tail special.

(4) A grant to a donee and the heirs of his or her body where no particular spouse was designated created a fee tail general.

b. Lineal heirs are sons, daughters, grandchildren, and great grandchildren. Collateral heirs are cousins, nieces, nephews, uncles, and aunts.

c. The fee tail estate is **not** freely alienable. The fee owner may only alienate the estate for the duration of his lifetime, at which time the estate passes to his lineal heir.

Example: O to A and the heirs of his (or her) body.

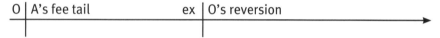

d. Since the estate may only pass to the lineal heirs of A, the estate may "expire" (ex) when there are no eligible lineal heirs of A remaining.

7. **Life Estate**

A life estate is a freehold estate where the duration is measured by the life or lives of one or more human beings.

Example: O to A for life.

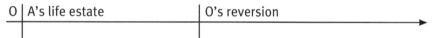

a. A life estate **pur autre vie** is a freehold estate where the duration is measured by the life of someone other than the grantee.

Example: O to A for the life of B.

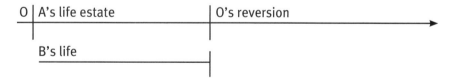

b. A life tenant is entitled to the beneficial use of the land, but he may not act to impair the value of the estates and interests owned by others in the same land.

c. A life tenant is not responsible for damage caused by others to the land. The life tenant may recover damages from third parties, for such damages, limited to the amount of interest of the life tenant.

d. A life tenant is **not** under a duty to insure the estate.

e. A life tenant is under a duty to **_pay interest on indebtedness_** that constitutes a lien on the property and to pay ordinary taxes as they accrue.

f. Assessments for permanent improvements are apportioned between the life tenant and the future interest holders.

B. FUTURE INTERESTS

1. Reversion

A reversion is the estate remaining in a grantor who has conveyed a lesser estate than that owned by the grantor.

Example: O to A and the heirs of his body.

| O | A's fee tail estate | O's reversion |

Example: O to A for life.

| O | A's life estate | O's reversion |

a. Generally, the owner of a freehold estate has a reversion if there is an outstanding lease. It is considered a possessory estate rather than a reversion if dower, curtesy, or the right to partition is involved.

b. An **_inter vivos_** conveyance of a possessory estate followed by a gift to the heirs or the next of kin of the conveyor presumably leaves a reversion in the conveyor. The **Doctrine of Worthier Title** forbids an owner to make an **_inter vivos_** conveyance to his heirs.

Example: O to A for life, remainder to O's heirs. Note that A has a life estate and the reversion is in the grantor.

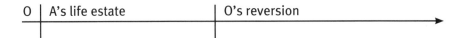

| O | A's life estate | O's reversion |

c. The rule has no application to a conveyance to a **_named person_** even if that person eventually turns out to be the heir of the grantor.

Example: O to A for life, remainder to my son, Richard. Note that a valid remainder in favor of Richard is created even if Richard is O's heir at O's death.

| O | A's life estate | Richard's remainder |

2. **Possibility of Reverter**

A possibility of reverter is the interest retained by the grantor of a determinable estate or a fee simple determinable. The possibility of reverter ripens into a possessory estate upon the occurrence of the named event. A change of conditions in the area may nullify the result triggered by the event.

Example: O to A and his heirs as long as the land is farmed.

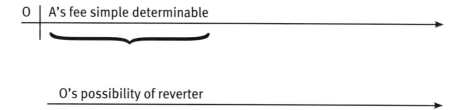

a. A possibility of reverter is alienable *inter vivos* and is subject to the general rules pertaining to testate and intestate succession.

b. Generally, the owner of a possibility of reverter is not entitled to share in a condemnation award if the proceedings involve a fee simple determinable.

3. **Power of Termination (Right of Entry)**

A power of termination (right of entry) is created in the grantor of an estate subject to a condition subsequent. Equitable relief may be available to prevent forfeiture in some circumstances.

Example: O to A and his heirs, but if the land is not farmed, then O may reenter and claim the land.

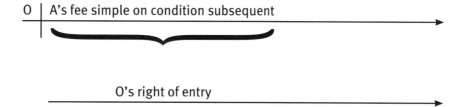

a. A legal action to recover the land is usually required.

b. The power of termination contained in a lease may be enforced by the party who acquires the reversion. The majority rule is that the power of termination is not alienable *inter vivos.*

c. The owner of a power of termination is not entitled to share in a condemnation proceedings award from the sale of an estate subject to a condition subsequent.

MULTISTATE NUANCE CHART:

FUTURE INTERESTS IN THE GRANTOR			
	REVERSION	**POSSIBILITY OF REVERTER**	**RIGHT OF ENTRY**
HOW IS THE INTEREST CREATED?	A reversion is created when the grantor conveys an expirable estate, *i.e.*, a fee tail, a life estate, or a contingent remainder that does not vest.	A possibility of reverter is created when the grantor conveys a fee simple determinable.	A right of entry is created when the grantor conveys a fee simple on condition subsequent.
IS THE INTEREST ALIENABLE?	Yes.	Yes.	No.
IS THE INTEREST INHERITABLE?	Yes.	Yes.	Yes.

4. **Remainders**

A remainder is a future interest created in a third person which is intended to take *after the natural termination* of a preceding estate. It must be created as part of the same grant which created a prior possessory estate, and the preceding estate must be smaller than a fee simple.

Example: O to A for life, then to B and his heirs.

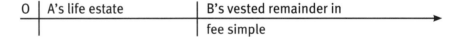

O	A's life estate	B's vested remainder in
		fee simple

Example: O to A for life, then if B survives A, to B and his heirs.

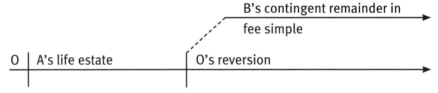

B's contingent remainder in
fee simple

| O | A's life estate | O's reversion |

a. **Creation:**

In the creation of a remainder the following elements must be present:

(1) the remainder must be in favor of a transferee who is one other than the conveyor,

(2) the remainder must be created at the same time and in the same instrument as the prior particular estate which supports it,

(3) the remainder must be so limited (described) that it will take effect as a present interest in possession immediately upon the termination of the prior particular estate, and

(4) the prior particular estate must be an estate of lesser duration than the interest of the conveyor at the time of the conveyance so that there can be an interest to pass in remainder.

b. **Nature of Preceding Estate**

At common law the particular estate which preceded and supported a remainder had to be a freehold estate, that is, either a fee tail or a life estate, but modern usage permits such prior estate to be either (1) a fee tail, (2) a life estate, or (3) an estate for years; it cannot be a fee simple estate.

c. **Types of Remainders**

Remainders are divided into two classes: vested remainders and contingent remainders.

(1) **Vested remainders:** A vested remainder is a remainder created in an ascertained and existing person that is not subject to any condition precedent except the normal termination of the preceding estate.

Examples:

In each case below C's remainder is *vested:*

A conveys or devises to B for life, then to C and her heirs;

To B and the heirs of her body, then to C and her heirs;

To B for life, then to C for life;

To B for life, then to X for life if she marries, remainder to C and her heirs;

To B for life, then to the children of X and their heirs (X being alive and having one child, C);

To B for life, then to C and her heirs but if C does not marry before B dies then to X and her heirs.

(2) **Types of vested remainders:**

(a) **Remainders absolutely vested:** A remainder is absolutely vested when it is limited to an ascertained or identifiable person or persons without words of condition and is not subject to divestment. Example: A conveys to B for life, then to C and her heirs. C has a remainder absolutely vested.

(b) **Remainders vested subject to partial divestment:** A remainder is vested subject to being partly divested when the remainderman is in existence and ascertained but the amount of her estate is subject to diminution in favor of other members of a class. This type of remainder, frequently called a *remainder vested subject to open,* is illustrated by a common kind of class gift. Example: A devises land to B for life, then to the children of B in fee. At the time of A's death B has one child, C. C's remainder is vested because she is in existence, ascertained, and she (or her heirs) is certain to acquire a possessory interest on the expiration of B's life estate. According to common law standards the seisin can pass to her immediately on B's death. But C's remainder is subject to open up and let in afterborn children of B because they also come within the terms of the gift. If after A's death two more children are born to B, they take equally with C as remaindermen and C's interest is reduced to a one-third share.

(c) **Remainders vested subject to complete divestment:** A remainder is vested subject to complete divestment when the remainderman is in existence and ascertained and her interest is not subject to a condition precedent, but her right to possession or enjoyment on the expiration of the prior interests is subject to termination by reason of (a) an executory interest, or (b) a power of appointment, or (c) a right of entry. Example: A conveys to B for life, then to C and her heirs, but if C dies leaving no surviving children then to D and his heirs. C has a remainder vested subject to complete divestment on the death of C without surviving children. D's interest is not a remainder but an executory interest.

(3) **Contingent remainders:** A contingent remainder is any remainder which is created in favor of an ascertained person but (a) *is subject to a condition precedent,* or (b) is created in favor of an *unborn person,* or (c) is created in favor of an existing but *unascertained person.*

Examples:

A to B for life, remainder to C and his heirs if C marries before B's death. C has a remainder contingent upon his marriage before B dies; or

A to B for life, remainder to C for life if C survives X. C has a remainder contingent upon X's predeceasing both B and C because the contingency of C's surviving X must happen on or before the termination of B's life estate.

(a) **Destructibility of contingent remainders:** At common law, a contingent remainder had to vest prior to termination of the preceding freehold estate or it was destroyed. Example: A to B for life, remainder to C and his heirs if C marries X. If C does not marry X before B dies, then the seisin will revert to A and C's contingent remainder is destroyed forever at common law. If he marries X but after B dies, that will not save or revive the irretrievably lost contingent remainder. Note: the destructibility rule is abolished in most but not all states.

(b) **Destructibility by merger:** Another situation in which a contingent remainder would fail by reason of the termination of the supporting life estate arose from the doctrine of merger of estates. By this doctrine, whenever successive vested estates are owned by the same person the smaller of the two estates will be absorbed by the larger. Example: If A conveys to B for life, then to B and his heirs, B has only one estate, a fee simple. By the doctrine of merger, the life estate merges in, or is swallowed by, the larger estate. By the same token, if A, owning in fee simple, conveys to B for life and A later transfers his reversion to B, the latter will have one estate—a fee simple, not a life estate but a reversion in fee. In order for a merger to take place the two estates must be successive and vested. Therefore, a merger will not be effected where a vested estate intervenes between the two estates.

(4) **Successive remainders:** More than one remainder may be designated to follow a freehold estate. Example: A to B for life, C for life, D for life, E for life, F for life, G and the heirs of his body. B has a life estate in possession. C has a vested remainder for life. Same as to D, E, and F. G has a vested remainder in fee tail. A has a reversion. It is immaterial that any one of the vested remainders for life may never be enjoyed by the remainderman such as E's dying before B, or that G may die without bodily heirs before B's life estate in possession terminates. The seisin will pass regularly to those named who are living and then revert to the grantor, A, or if he be dead the reversion will have descended to his heirs.

(5) **Characteristics of remainders:**

(a) **Alienable:** Today, all remainders are considered alienable, devisable, and descendable. At common law, remainders were considered *in*alienable (i.e., non-transferable).

(b) **Creditors:** A contingent remainder is not subject to claims of creditors although vested remainders are.

(c) **When it takes effect:** A remainder cannot take effect in derogation of, that is by cutting short, the prior particular estate; it can take effect only when such prior particular estate comes to an end naturally according to its limitation. Example: A conveys "to B for life, then to C and his heirs." C has a vested remainder which takes effect after the natural expiration of B's life estate. Conversely, an *executory interest* "cuts short" a prior estate.

(d) **Rule Against Perpetuities:** A vested remainder, being vested, is *not* subject to the R ule Against Perpetuities; a contingent remainder is subject to the Rule.

MULTISTATE NUANCE CHART:

VESTED REMAINDER	CONTINGENT REMAINDER
1. Is vested.	1. Is *not* vested.
2. Is *not* subject to the Rule Against Perpetuities.	2. Is subject to the Rule Against Perpetuities.
3. Is limited to an ascertained person who has the right to immediate possession if and when the prior estate is terminated.	3. Is subject to a condition precedent; it will not vest until the happening of an event or the ascertainment of a person.
4. Remainderman has right against prior estate owner (e.g., life tenant) for waste.	4. Remainderman has *no* right against prior estate owner (e.g., life tenant) for waste.
5. Remainderman has right to compel prior estate owner to pay taxes and interest on encumbrances.	5. Remainderman *cannot* compel estate owner to pay taxes or interest on encumbrances.

5. **Executory Interests**

   An executory interest is a future contingent interest created in favor of a transferee under the Statute of Uses (1535) or Statute of Wills (1540) in the form of a ***springing or shifting use*** which, on the happening of the contingency described, will be executed into a legal estate, and which cannot be construed as a remainder.

   a. **Elements Essential to Creation of an Executory Interest:**

      (1) It is always in favor of a transferee, one other than the transferor. As such, an executory interest should never be confused with a reversion, a possibility of reverter, or a right of entry for condition broken.

      (2) It is always contingent and can never become vested, because when it vests whether as a future or present interest, it ceases to be an executory interest.

      (3) It must take effect either (a) before the natural termination of the preceding estate, therefore in derogation thereof or by divesting it, or (b) after the termination of the preceding estate.

   b. **Shifting Executory Interests Divest Transferees**

      A shifting executory interest "cuts short" or terminates a preceding estate in favor of another grantee. Example: A conveys to B for life but if B becomes bankrupt then to C and his heirs. The state of title is life estate in B subject to an executory (shifting) interest in C, reversion in A. Note that C's interest is not a remainder because it does not await the natural expiration of B's life estate, but instead may cut it short.

(1) A *shifting executory interest* shifts the right to possession from one grantee to another grantee.

c. Springing Executory Interests Divest Grantors

A *springing executory interest* is an estate created to begin *in futuro* and "cuts short" or terminates a reversion held by the grantor. Example: A conveys to B for life, and one year after B's death to C and his heirs. The state of the title is life estate in B, reversion in fee simple to A subject to an executory (springing) interest in C to take effect in possession one year after B's death.

d. Distinction Between "Shifting" and "Springing" Interests

A shifting executory interest "cuts short" a prior estate created in favor of another grantee. For example, A conveys "to B and his heirs but if B marries Z, then to C and his heirs." In the event B marries Z, B's fee is cut off and title shifts to C. On the other hand, a *springing executory interest "cuts short" an estate held by the grantor*. For example, A conveys "to B for life and one year after B's death to C and his heirs." In this situation, B is given a life estate, which is followed by a reversion in fee to A for one year, then a springing use in C.

Caveat: The best way to distinguish between shifting and springing uses is to remember that title passes as follows:

Shifting Use: Grantor to 1st Grantee to 2nd Grantee

Springing Use: Grantor to 1st Grantee to Grantor to 2nd Grantee

e. Distinction Between Executory Interests and Contingent Remainders

A *contingent remainder cannot follow a fee simple interest* of any kind. Therefore, *any interest which follows a fee and is held by a third person must be an executory interest*. For example, A conveys "to B and his heirs but if B sells liquor on the premises, then to C and his heirs." C has a shifting executory interest. It is obvious that C's interest cannot be a contingent remainder because (1) a remainder cannot follow a fee simple and (2) a remainder cannot "cut short" a preceding vested estate.

f. Distinction Between Executory Interests and Devises

Executory devises are identical with springing and shifting executory interests except executory devises are *created by will* whereas springing and shifting uses are *created by grant or deed inter vivos*.

Question:

Smith's will would devise Monicacre "to my friend, Monte, to whom I am everlastingly grateful for the devoted care he has lavished on my horses, but if ever my horses who survive me shall fail to receive proper care, then to my beloved daughter, Doris and her heirs, if she be living and own any horses; otherwise to the Malibu Equestrian Society."

In an appropriate action to construe the will, the court will determine Monte's interest to be a (an)

(A) fee simple determinable
(B) fee simple subject to condition subsequent
(C) fee simple subject to an executory interest
(D) contingent remainder

Answer:

(C) It is important to note that Doris has an executory devise. The characteristics of this interest are exactly the same as those that attach to springing and shifting uses. Note that the devise is created by will and not by deed. Doris' interest cannot be a remainder for two reasons: (1) a *remainder cannot follow a fee simple,* and (2) a remainder cannot come in and cut short the preceding vested estate. In this case, Monte has a fee simple subject to an executory devise in Doris.

6. **Rule in Shelley's Case (Rule Against Remainders in Grantee's Heirs)**

At common law, if in a conveyance or a will a freehold estate (usually a life estate) is given to a person and in the same conveyance or will a remainder is limited to the heirs or to the heirs of the body of that person, that person takes both the freehold estate and the remainder. The effect of the rule is to convert what would otherwise be a remainder in the heirs or heirs of the body into a remainder in the ancestor.

Example: A conveys or devises land to B for life, and after B's death to the heirs of B. Apart from the Rule in Shelley's Case the state of the title would be as follows: life estate in B, contingent remainder in fee simple in B's heirs, reversion in A in fee. But by application of the Rule, the state of title is as such: life estate in B, vested remainder in B in fee simple. The doctrine of merger will thus cause B's life estate to merge with his remainder so that the ultimate result is that B gets a present estate in fee simple.

Example: In like manner, if A grants or devises to B for life, remainder to the heirs of B's body, by virtue of the Rule plus the operation of merger, B, at common law, gets a present estate in fee tail.

a. **Requirements:** In order for the Rule to apply the following requirements must be satisfied:

(1) there must be a freehold estate (e.g., *life estate*) given to the grantee or devisee;

(2) by the same instrument, *a remainder must be limited to the heirs* or heirs of the body of the grantee or devisee; and

(3) the freehold and the remainder must be of the same quality, that is, both legal or both equitable.

b. **Rule Abolished in Most States:** Thirty-six states and the District of Columbia have abolished the Rule either wholly or in part. In some states the wording of the

statute is such as not to cover explicitly all situations to which the Rule might be applicable and a question may arise as to the scope of the statute. At the present time, however, the Rule still exists in Arkansas, Colorado, Delaware, Indiana, North Carolina, and Texas.

7. **The Doctrine of Worthier Title (The Rule Against Remainders in Grantor's Heirs)**

At common law, a man could not either by conveyance or by devise limit a fee simple to his own heirs. The heirs of the transferor were not permitted to take as purchasers under the conveyance or will and the attempted limitation was void.

Example: A, owner of land in fee simple, devises it to B for life, then to the heirs of A. The *remainder* to the heirs of A is *void* as such and they take the *reversion by descent.*

a. **Application to Inter Vivos Transfers**

The rule in its application to inter vivos transfers came to this: *a conveyor cannot create a remainder in his own heirs.* In the case of a conveyance the effect of the rule is to convert what would otherwise be a contingent remainder in the heirs of the conveyor into a reversion in the conveyor himself. Thus, A conveys to B for life, and after B's death to the heirs of A. By virtue of the rule the state of title is this: life estate in B, reversion in fee simple in A.

b. **Application to Wills**

Where a will devised to the heirs of the testator an estate of the same kind and quality as the heirs would have taken by descent if the devisor had died intestate, the heirs were required to take by descent instead of by purchase. Thus, A, owner of land in fee simple, devises it to B for life, then to the heirs of A. The remainder to the heirs of A is void as such and they take the reversion by descent.

(1) **"Worthier" method of descent:** The rule in its testamentary aspect required the heir to take by descent rather than by devise, and *title by descent* was said to be "worthier" or better than a title derived by purchase for the reason that a descent of land from a disseisor to his heir barred the right of entry of the person disseised, whereas if the title were acquired by purchase the disseisee's entry was not barred.

c. **The Doctrine in American Law:** In a substantial number of states the Doctrine of Worthier Title in both of its branches (i.e., inter vivos transfers and devises) has been recognized and accepted as a part of the common law. In recent years, however, there has been a *trend* in the direction of statutory abrogation of the rule. Statutes abolishing the doctrine have been enacted in California, Illinois, Kansas (wills only), Minnesota, and Nebraska, to name a few.

8. **Rule Against Perpetuities**

Definition: No interest is good unless it must vest, if at all, not later than twenty-one years after some life in being at the creation of the interest.

a. **"No interest is good"** means that *any contingent interest* which does not conform to the rule is void ab initio.

b. **"Must vest"** means that the contingent interest must become a vested interest (or fail) within the period of the rule.

   Example: If A conveys to B for life, remainder to the heirs of C, and C predeceases B, the contingent remainder becomes a vested remainder. The rule is satisfied by a vesting in interest even though possession is postponed.

c. **"If at all"** means that if the contingent interest is absolutely certain either to "vest" or "fail" entirely within the period of the rule, it is valid.

d. **"Not later than 21 years after some life in being"** includes within the period (1) lives in being, provided they are not so numerous as to prevent practical determination of the time when the last one dies, plus (2) 21 years, plus (3) such actual periods of gestation as come within the proper purpose of the rule.

   Example: A, fee owner, by deed conveys to B for life, then to the first child of C who attains the age of 21 years whether that be before or after the death of B. At the time of the conveyance C is a living single person having no child. Are all the interests valid under the common law rule? The answer is yes.

   Analysis: First, since the interest of C's child is contingent there is a reversion in A subject to being divested. Note, however, that every reversion is vested and therefore the rule has no application to A's reversion. Secondly, B's interest is presently vested in possession and the rule does not apply to it. Thirdly, with respect to the interest of C's first child to attain the age of 21, it is contingent both on his being born and surviving to the age of 21. The question is whether there is any possibility that this interest will vest later than a life in being and 21 years. The answer is no. The reason is because the measuring life is C. No child can be born to C later than the period of gestation (normally 9 months is allowed) after C's death. Any such child must attain the age of 21 years, if at all, within 21 years after its birth. So the longest possible time when such interest must either vest or fail is C's life plus a period of gestation plus 21 years. Under the rule *a child in the womb is in being*. Therefore, the rule does not invalidate any interest because the period stated is extended by an actual period of gestation. Hence, the interest of C's first child who may attain the age of 21 must either vest or fail within the allowable period and there is no possibility that it can vest at any later time. Thus, it is valid.

e. **"At the creation of the interest"** means that in the ordinary case the period of the rule begins when the creating instrument (e.g., will or deed) takes effect.

f. **Rule Directed Against Remoteness of Vesting:** The rule is directed entirely against remoteness of vesting, i.e., the sole test is whether, the interest *must* vest (or fail) within the period of the rule. If it *may* vest beyond the maximum period permitted by the rule, it is void.

   (1) **Purpose:** While the rule is directed toward remoteness of vesting, its ultimate purpose is to prevent the clogging of titles beyond reasonable limits in time by contingent interests and to keep land freely alienable in the market places.

g. **Interests Subject to Rule:**

   (1) *contingent remainders*

   (2) *executory interests*

   (3) *options to purchase land not incident to a lease*

   (4) *powers of appointment*

   (5) *rights of first refusal*

   (6) *class gifts*

h. **Interests *Not* Subject to the Rule:**

   (1) present interests in possession

   (2) reversions

   (3) vested remainders

   (4) possibilities of reverter

   (5) powers of termination

   (6) charitable trusts

   (7) resulting trusts

i. **The "Measuring Life":** Under the rule, *lives in being must be:*

   (1) human lives, not the lives of any of the lower animals or lives of corporations;

   (2) the lives in being must precede, they cannot follow, the 21 years;

   (3) every human being is conclusively presumed capable of having children during her lifetime;

   Example: A, being fee simple owner of Blackacre, devised it "to the children of B for their lives and the life of the survivor of them, then to B's grandchildren in fee simple." At the time A dies, B is a woman of the age of 85 and she has three children, X, Y, and Z. There is a residuary clause in M's favor. When the survivor of X, Y, and Z dies M takes possession of Blackacre and sues to quiet title in himself. Will he succeed? The answer is yes.

   Analysis: Every living person is conclusively presumed capable of having children as long as she lives. So it must be kept in mind that even though B is 85 years of age she can legally have children until her death, regardless of the fact that biologically she may be quite incapable of reproduction. Hence, it is legally possible that B may have another child, H, who will have children who will qualify as B's grandchildren and who were not in being at A's death and may not come into being until more than 21 years after the deaths of X,

Y, and Z. It is possible then that all of B's children and grandchildren except H's children, who were not "lives in being at the creation of the interest," will have dropped out before the interest created by A's devise will vest, and that H's children will be the only ones who can take such interest. This provision fetters the alienation of Blackacre for a longer time than is permitted under the rule, thus making the gift "to B's grandchildren in fee simple" absolutely void ab initio.

Exam Tip: In such cases there is often a thin line between what is valid and what is void. Notice in this case, had A's will limited B's grandchildren to the "children of X, Y, and Z," then the devise to such grandchildren would have been valid because the lives in being as measuring lives would have been X, Y, and Z, and their children were bound to take vested interests not later than the death of the survivor of X, Y, and Z and a period of gestation, from the "creation of the interest."

(4) the lives in the measuring group or class must **not be so numerous** or so situated that the survivor cannot be practically determined by the ordinary evidentiary processes, e.g., if the lives in being were all the persons now living in the state of California, or in Great Britain, the interest would be void.

j. **Time for Vesting:** The time for vesting is generally calculated from the time the creating instrument takes effect. In the case of a will, it is the **date of the testator's death;** whereas in a **deed,** it is the time of **delivery.**

Example: A, being fee owner, devises Blackacre "to the children of my son, B, who reach the age of 25." At A's death, B has four sons ranging in age from 14 to 22. B dies 10 days after the death of A, leaving no other children. Is the devise to the children valid under the Rule Against Perpetuities? The answer is no.

Analysis: The validity of an interest created by a will must be determined as of the date when the will takes effect, that is in our case at A's death. Looking forward from that date these possibilities, and we are dealing with possibilities not probabilities, must be observed. First, as long as B lives he is conclusively presumed capable of having more children. Second, it is possible that he will have other children after A's death. Third, it is possible that all of B's four sons living at A's death will die before any one of them arrives at the age of 25. Fourth, then it is possible that the only one, if any, of B's children who will arrive at the age of 25 will be a child who is born after A's will took effect. Fifth, it is possible that such child may be born posthumously, that is, after the death of B and that it will take 25 more years for him to arrive at the required age for an interest in Blackacre to vest in him. In conclusion, it is possible that any interest in B's children will vest at a time later than any life in being and 21 years after the will of A took effect. Consequently, the devise in favor of B's children who reach the age of 25 violates the rule and is void ab initio.

9. **Class Gifts (Remainders Subject to Open)**

If a remainder interest is given to a class of persons, it is deemed vested only when the class is closed and all conditions precedent for every member of the class have been

satisfied. *The entire class gift is void if the interest of one member might possibly violate the rule.* However, some jurisdictions protect these gifts by a "rule of convenience" which treats a class as closed at distribution to any member of it entitled to demand his share.

a. **Class Closing Rule:** A class is closed when no one born after that date can share in the gift. A class can close physiologically or under the "rule of convenience."

   (1) **Physiological closing:** A class closes physiologically when the parent of the class dies. As such, a gift to A's children would close physiologically at A's death.

   (2) **Closing under the "rule of convenience":** By applying the "rule of convenience," however, a class can close earlier. Whenever any member of the class is entitled *to demand possession* of his share, the class closes. By this method, gifts can often be saved from violating the Rule Against Perpetuities.

   Example: "To Margo for life and then to her surviving children when they reach the age of 25." Margo could have another child, who would not turn 25 until more than 21 years after the death of all the other parties. That possibility invalidates the gift to all children even those living, unless the rule of convenience is applied to save it and there is one child who is 25 when she dies.

   Example: A, being fee owner, devises Blackacre "to B for life, then to B's grandchildren in fee." If there is one grandchild of B alive at A's death, the gift to the grandchildren is valid. It is certain at A's death that the class will close at B's death because that grandchild will demand possession of his share at B's death. Conversely, if there is no grandchild of B alive at A's death, it is not certain that the class will close at B's death, and the gift is void.

10. **Powers of Appointment**

   a. **General Power of Appointment**

   A general power of appointment is considered the equivalent of ownership of property. Hence, if one has a general power of appointment over property he can exercise such power and alienate the property. Thus, if one can alienate the property the Rule Against Perpetuities is not offended. So, in order for a general power to be valid under the rule it must be exercisable, but not necessarily exercised, during the period allowed by the rule.

   b. **Special Power of Appointment**

   A special power of appointment is not the equivalent of property because it must be either exercised in a limited way or in favor of a limited class of persons. To be valid under the Rule Against Perpetuities, a special power of appointment is required to be exercised so that the interest in property thereby created will vest within the period of the rule. If it is possible to exercise a special power of appointment later than a life in being and 21 years after its creation, then the power is void from its inception.

11. **Restraints on Alienation**

Restraints on alienation are provisions in deeds, wills, and mortgages that restrict the grantee's power to convey property to others. Whether the particular restraint will be valid depends upon the kind of restraint, the estate restrained, and the extent of the restraint.

a. **The Estate Restrained**

(1) **Fee simple interests:** As a general rule, any direct restraint imposed upon a fee simple is *invalid;* only estates less than fees may be subject to restraints upon their alienation. In a few states direct restraints on fees which are only partial are upheld.

(2) **Concurrent estates:** Restrictions limiting the power of joint tenants or tenants in common to seek partition are usually upheld. Such provisions appear in the deeds or by-laws of most condominiums and cooperatives.

(3) **Lesser estates:** Restraints on alienation of nonfreehold estates are commonly upheld. The *non-assignment clause* in a lease is a common example.

b. **The Type of Restraint**

(1) **Disabling:** A disabling restraint seeks to withhold the power of alienation (e.g., "shall not transfer" or "any transfer is void").

(2) **Forfeiture:** A forfeiture restraint provides that the grantor may terminate the estate if a conveyance is made (usually by use of a condition subsequent).

(3) **Promissory:** A promissory restraint consists of the grantee's promise (covenant) not to alienate.

(a) **Validity of restraints:** Disabling restraints on alienation are always void, even when less than a freehold estate is involved. Forfeiture restraints are automatically invalid only where a fee is involved; if lesser estates are involved they may be upheld. Promissory restraints may or may not be valid depending upon the other variables.

c. **Extent of Restraint**

A restraint may be total or partial. A partial restraint restricts the grantee only in some particular respect:

(1) **Time:** A restraint may only limit the grantee for a limited period of time. While a disabling restraint is always void, a forfeiture or promissory restraint may be valid if it is limited in time.

(2) **Persons:** A restraint may prohibit the grantee from conveying to certain persons (e.g., racial minorities). When such restraints are used to discriminate against religious, racial or social groups, they are held *invalid* under the Fourteenth Amendment.

(3) **Preemptive rights:** The inclusion of a *right of first refusal* in a deed instrument constitutes a partial restraint on alienation. Such restraints are usually valid provided they do not violate the Rule Against Perpetuities.

C. CONCURRENT ESTATES

1. Joint Tenancy

A joint tenancy is a form of co-ownership where each tenant owns an undivided interest in the whole estate. Its distinguishing feature is the right of survivorship, which means that upon the death of one joint tenant, the surviving tenant or tenants own the whole of the property and nothing passes to the heirs of the decedent.

a. **Creation:** At common law, four unities were required to create a joint tenancy:

(1) Unity of *time* (interests vested at the same time);

(2) Unity of *title* (interests acquired by the same instrument);

(3) Unity of *interest* (interests of the same type and duration); and

(4) Unity of *possession* (interests give identical rights of enjoyment).

b. **Modern View:** Modernly, not all jurisdictions require the four unities. In many jurisdictions, an owner need not use a straw man so that the unities of time and title are satisfied. Rather, she can convey simply to herself and to another person as joint tenants.

c. **Requirements**

(1) Joint tenancy is always created by deed or by will, never by descent.

(2) In joint tenancy there must always be two or more grantees or devisees.

d. **Express language required:** Under modern law, joint tenancies are disfavored. Consequently, there must be a clear expression of intent to create this estate; otherwise it will not be recognized.

Example: *A "to B and C and their heirs" are typical words for creating a joint tenancy at common law.* Today, in the absence of a clearly expressed intent to create a joint tenancy with the right of survivorship, such a grant creates a tenancy in common.

MBE Exam Tip: In answering an MBE Property question dealing with joint tenancy, apply the common law rule unless the facts state otherwise.

e. **Termination**

(1) **Inter vivos conveyance by one joint tenant:** A conveyance inter vivos *severs the joint tenancy so that the transferee takes the interest as a tenant in common* and not as a joint tenant.

Question:

Johnny and Joanna Appleseed married in 1955. Two years later, they acquired ownership to Marshacre "as joint tenants with right of survivorship." Marshacre was comprised mostly of swampland and was located five miles outside of Secaucus. When the Appleseeds purchased the property, it had little monetary value and was not very desirable. Recently, however, the state conducted a large scale land-fill operation of the swampland. This made Marshacre suitable for residential lots and resulted in the commercial development of the area. As a consequence, the market value of Marshacre increased substantially.

In 1985, the Appleseeds wished to convey an interest in Marshacre to their daughter, Joy, and her husband, Joshua. Thereupon, Johnny and Joanna executed a deed wherein they conveyed an undivided 15 percent interest in Marshacre to Joy. In 1988, the Appleseeds then conveyed a 15 percent interest in Marshacre to Joshua. The common-law joint tenancy is unmodified by statute, and the jurisdiction in which Marshacre is located does not require tenancy by the entirety or community property.

Title to Marshacre is in Johnny and Joanna Appleseed as

- (A) joint tenants as to 70 percent, Joy as a tenant in common as to 15 percent, and Joshua as a tenant in common as to 15 percent
- (B) joint tenants as to 70 percent and Joy and Joshua as joint tenants as to 30 percent
- (C) tenants in common as to 70 percent, Joy as a tenant in common as to 15 percent, and Joshua as a tenant in common as to 15 percent
- (D) tenants in common as to 70 percent and Joy and Joshua as joint tenants as to 30 percent

Answer:

(A) As a general rule, any conveyance inter vivos by a joint tenant constitutes a complete severance of her interest in the jointly owned property and destroys the joint tenancy *as to the extent of the interest conveyed*. Thus, by conveying 30% of Marshacre to Joy and Joshua, the joint tenancy was destroyed with respect to that portion of the property. However, the joint tenancy interest still applies to the 70% tract of Marshacre retained by Johnny and Joanna. Choice (A) is correct because as to the undivided 70% interest Johnny and Joanna remain joint tenants, while Joy and Joshua are tenants in common to their individual 15% interests.

(2) **Partition:** A partition occurs when a dispute arises between co-tenants about the property. In this situation, the co-tenants may wish to have the property divided by an equity court so that they no longer have to share possession and ownership of the property. A joint tenancy is destroyed by a final partition decree of an equity court. Suit for partition may be brought by any joint tenant.

Note: Simply filing suit for partition is not enough, because the parties may settle their difference while the partition proceeding is pending. Therefore, *severance requires a final partition decree*.

(3) **Mortgages:** In a *minority of states* that follow a "title theory," a mortgage is regarded as a transfer of title and thus causes a severance.

   (a) **Majority view:** A mortgage is regarded as *a lien on title*, and one joint tenant's execution of a mortgage does not by itself result in a severance. However, a severance does occur in the event that the mortgage is foreclosed and the property is subsequently sold.

(4) **Leases:** According to the majority rule, a lease does not effectuate a termination of a joint tenancy.

   (a) **Death of lessor/joint tenant:** In a majority of states, because the lessor's own right to possession would cease on her death, so must the right of any lessee.

(5) **Contract to convey:** In most states, a contract to convey results in a severance of a joint tenancy (despite the fact that no actual transfer of title has been made).

   Rationale: The contract to convey is enforceable in *equity*, and thus it is treated as an effective transfer of an equitable interest. Therefore, if the vendor dies before the title is transferred, the vendee is entitled to a deed from the vendor's estate and becomes a tenant in common with the original joint tenant(s).

(6) **Judgment liens:** A judgment lien arises when judgment is rendered against a landowner defendant. In this situation, the successful plaintiff will hold a lien on any property the defendant owns in the county where the judgment was rendered. This lien becomes a burden on the land until the landowner defendant pays the judgment. Where a plaintiff obtains such a lien against one joint tenant and not against the others, it generally does not severe a joint tenancy, because it does not settle the unities of time and title. Of course, if the lien is not paid and the plaintiff attempts to satisfy the judgment through foreclosure, there will be a severance.

(7) **Effect of gift in will by a joint tenant:** Where a joint tenant attempts to devise her interest in property to her heirs, such a gift is ineffective both at the time the will is written and at the joint tenant's death. It is ineffective at the time it is written because the will does not operate until the testator dies, and therefore no severance occurs. Of course, it is not an effective gift upon the joint tenant's death, because the joint tenants take the testator's share immediately upon the testator's death through the right of survivorship, and nothing is left to pass onto the heirs.

   (a) **Agreement to devise:** Occasionally, all joint tenants will enter into an agreement whereby one joint tenant may devise his share. In this situation, a devise will be valid, in that the agreement itself severs the joint tenancy.

2. **Tenancy by the Entirety**

A tenancy by the entirety is a form of co-ownership similar to a joint tenancy based upon the common law concept of *unity of husband and wife*. Tenancy by the entirety

is a species of joint tenancy, and, like in joint tenancy, each spouse owns the whole estate and not a fractional part thereof.

a. **Right of Survivorship:** Just as in a joint tenancy, the doctrine of survivorship operates in a tenancy by the entirety so that the survivor spouse takes the whole estate and the heirs receive nothing.

b. **Unities:** Five unities are essential in a tenancy by the entirety:

(1) *Time,*

(2) *Title,*

(3) *Interest,*

(4) *Possession,* and

(5) *Person* (i.e., unity of husband and wife).

c. **Severance**

(1) **Conveyance:** In most states, neither spouse can individually dispose of any interest in the estate by entireties; rather, *both must join in the conveyance.*

(2) *Death of either spouse*

(3) *Divorce eliminates the unity of person* and destroys the tenancy by entirety. The divorced persons become tenants in common.

(4) *Execution by a joint creditor of both husband and wife* (but a creditor of *one spouse* cannot levy upon the estate owned by the entirety).

(5) **Partition:** Because the tenancy by entirety is to protect the family, *neither spouse has a right to have partition,* and neither has the power, without the consent of the other, to destroy such tenancy.

(6) **Mutual Agreement:** Where both spouses agree to destroy the tenancy by the entirety, such an agreement will be effective.

d. **Community Property States:** Note that, in community property states, tenancies by the entirety are not recognized.

e. **Presumption of Tenancy by the Entirety:** In about 21 jurisdictions, where a conveyance is made to a husband and wife, the estate is assumed to be held as a tenancy by the entirety.

3. **Tenancy in Common**

A tenancy in common is a concurrent estate in which co-tenants each own an undivided, *separate and distinct share* of the property. It is important to note that a tenant in common does not own the whole property as in a joint tenancy. Each tenant can

dispose of her undivided fractional part or any portion thereof, either by deed or will. The only "unity" is that of *possession* inasmuch as each tenant is entitled to possession of the whole estate.

a. **No Right of Survivorship:** Upon the death intestate of a tenant in common, her interest *descends to her heirs*. There is *no right of survivorship*.

b. **Destruction**

   (1) **Partition:** A tenancy in common may be destroyed by partition.

   (2) **Merger:** A tenancy in common is destroyed by merger when the entire title vests in one person, either by purchase or otherwise.

c. **Conveyance:** This interest *is freely alienable* by inter vivos and testamentary transfer.

d. **Ouster:** An ouster occurs where one co-tenant manages *to wrongfully exclude his co-tenants from possession* of the property. When one co-tenant ousts from possession her co-tenant, the ousted tenant has a cause of action against the possessor, not to put her out, but to regain possession for herself with the possessor. Where one co-tenant stakes a claim for exclusive possession of any part of the property, the claim alone may amount to an ouster.

e. **Fiduciary Relationship:** There is *no real fiduciary relationship between co-tenants* merely because of the co-tenancy, but good faith between co-tenants prevents one co-tenant from buying up an adverse title and asserting it against her co-tenants if such co-tenants offer to share their part of the expense of gaining such title. The buyer of such adverse title is said to hold in *constructive trust* for her co-tenants.

f. **Right to Possession:** Because each co-tenant has an undivided interest in the property, each has a right to possession of the entire property. However, note that no individual co-tenant has a right to exclusive possession to any portion of the property.

g. **Encumbrance on the Property:** Where one co-tenant encumbers the property with a mortgage, this mortgage does not affect the other co-tenant's interests. Therefore, if a foreclosure occurs, the mortgagee may only foreclose on the interest of the co-tenant who took out the mortgage.

4. **Rights and Duties of Tenants by the Entirety, Joint Tenants, or Tenants in Common**

a. **Possession:** In all forms of concurrent ownership, each tenant has the right to possess and enjoy the whole estate.

b. **Rents and Profits:** In a *majority of states*, a tenant in possession has the right to retain profits gained by *her use* of the property. By the same token, a tenant in possession need not share such profits with a co-tenant out of possession, nor reimburse him for the rental value of her use of the land, *unless there has been an ouster*. However, a co-tenant out of possession has a right to share in rents and profits received from *third parties*.

c. **Taxes:** A tenant who has paid the entire taxes on the property may either compel contribution by her co-tenants or enforce a lien against the property for such. Contribution may also be compelled for mortgage payments made by one co-tenant, as long as the co-tenant making the payments is not in sole possession of the property. Where she is in sole possession of the property, the court will only reimburse her if the payments she has made are in excess of the amount the property would net if rented.

d. **Repairs and Improvements**

(1) **Majority Rule – Repairs:** The majority rule states that a co-tenant who spends his own money to make necessary repairs to the property can require that the other co-tenants contribute to the cost of such repairs. The general rule is that the co-tenant making the repairs and laying out the money must notify the other co-tenants in advance of the necessity of such repairs and of the co-tenant's expected contribution.

(2) **Minority Rule – Repairs:** A tenant has *no right of contribution against the other co-tenant(s) for repairs* he has made, but if *partition* is had, the court in making an equitable division of the proceeds will take into consideration the expenditures made by one tenant for repairs and improvements.

(3) **Improvements:** A co-tenant who makes improvements to the property is not entitled to contribution from other co-tenants. If a partition occurs, then the court may "even up" the expenses paid by reimbursing the co-tenant who made the improvements.

II. LANDLORD AND TENANT

A. NATURE OF LEASEHOLD

1. **Conveyance**

   A lease involves the conveyance of an estate in land and thus is subject to the Statute of Frauds. To satisfy the Statute of Frauds requirements, the writing must:

   a. *identify the lessor and the lessee;*

   b. *describe the leased land;*

   c. *state the term of the lease; and,*

   d. *set forth the amount of rent.*

2. **Contract**

   Modern leases also contain many covenants (e.g., quiet enjoyment) that impose *contractual obligations* on the part of the landlord and tenant. Consequently, most courts treat leases more as contracts than as conveyances. In so doing, the modern trend is

to apply contract, rather than property, principles with respect to the landlord-tenant relationship.

B. TENANT DUTIES

1. **Duty to Pay Rent:** Today, rent is the ***consideration*** paid by a tenant to her landlord for the use and enjoyment of the land. The amount of rent is determined by the agreement between the landlord and tenant and is contractual in nature.

   a. **When Rent Accrues:** At common law rent is not apportionable as to time. It does ***not accrue from day to day*** as does interest on money loaned. Under the common law, if a lease provides for the payment of annual rent on the last day of the calendar year and the lessor accepts a surrender of the leasehold any time during the year, she can collect no rent for any portion of such year. Modernly, however, most jurisdictions now require that a tenant pay the pro-rated amount for any term he is in possession, less than the term stated in the lease.

   b. **Destruction of Premises:** At common law a ***tenant remains liable to pay rent*** even though because of fire, floods, storms or other action of the elements or otherwise, the property is rendered totally uninhabitable, unless the lease otherwise provides.

   c. **Rent Extinguished or Suspended By:**

      (1) **Release by the landlord**

      (2) **Merger**

         Example: L, fee simple owner of Blackacre, leases it to T for 10 years at a rent of $200 per month. L dies intestate during the term, and T is her sole heir. The reversion and the rent incident thereto and the leasehold of T are all merged in the fee simple;

      (3) **Expiration of the lease**

      (4) **Eminent Domain that Takes Both the Leasehold and the Reversion**

         (a) **Entire leasehold taken by eminent domain:** If all the leased land is condemned for the full balance of the lease term, the tenant's liability for rent is extinguished.

         (b) **Temporary or partial taking:** If the taking is temporary (i.e., for a period less than the remaining term), or if only a portion of the leased property is condemned, the tenant is not discharged from her obligation to pay rent.

      (5) **Constructive eviction:** *A material breach by the landlord which violates the tenant's implied covenant of quiet enjoyment constitutes a constructive eviction if it renders the premises uninhabitable* and the tenant quits the premises in a timely fashion.

Example: Landlord, owner of a dwelling, leased it to Tenant. Shortly after Tenant took possession, Landlord changed the heating system in the home from one operated by coal to oil. For two months following the changeover, soot, smoke, and oil fumes came through the floor and baseboards in the dwelling to such an extent that Tenant's physician advised her to vacate the premises to preserve her health. Landlord, who was notified of the condition, failed to correct the problem, and Tenant vacated the premises. Landlord has constructively evicted tenant by violating the implied covenant of quiet enjoyment.

(6) **Frustration of purpose:** The complete, or almost complete, frustration of purpose as, for example, when the sole use provided for in the lease becomes illegal.

(7) **Surrender:** A surrender, either by express agreement or by operation of law. Where a tenant fails to pay rent, a landlord may generally either evict the tenant or sue the tenant for the rent payments owed.

2. **Duty to Repair:** A tenant cannot damage (i.e., ***commit waste*** on) the leased premises.

   a. **Voluntary Waste:** This consists of injury to the premises or land caused by an intentional or negligent affirmative act of the tenant (either life tenant or tenant for years), such as exploiting minerals on the land unless the property was previously so used or the lease so provided.

   b. **Ameliorating Waste:** This consists of ***a change in the physical characteristics of the occupied premises by an unauthorized act of the tenant which increases the value of the land***. At common law, a tenant was not allowed to substantially alter leased property, even if in so doing she substantially increased the value of the property. Where she made changes, the landlord was entitled to be reimbursed for the amount he would have had to pay to restore the building to its original condition, even though that original condition was worse than the improved condition the tenant had created. However, under the modern view, a tenant will not be liable for ameliorative waste if the improvements actually increased the value of the premises, the tenant is one who has possessed the premises for a long period of time, and the changes are consistent with similar changes in the neighborhood.

   Example: Tenant razes an old and outmoded building on the leased premises and builds a modern building that increases the value of the land from $10,000 to $50,000. Under modern law, the tenant will not be liable to the landlord for restoration, if the building is in line with the character of other buildings in the neighborhood and if this tenant has possessed the building for a long period of time.

   c. **Permissive Waste:** This consists of injury to the premises or land caused by the tenant's failure to act when it is her duty to act (e.g., there is a hole in the roof of a leased dwelling house which tenant fails to repair, thus causing rain to leak and damaging the hardwood floors of the house). The tenant is under a ***duty to make ordinary repairs***. While the landlord retains the duty to make ***substantial repairs***, the tenant does possess a duty to report the need for such repairs to the landlord in a reasonable time.

d. **Equitable Waste:** This consists of injury to the reversionary interest in land, which is inconsistent with good husbandry. It is recognized only by the equity courts and does not constitute legal waste. It usually arises when the expression "without impeachment of waste" appears in the lease, which means that the life tenant or tenant for years may use the leased premises as a fee simple owner might use the land.

Example: At law a fee simple owner may raze his hotel building and build a dwelling house on the land. But because no reasonable fee owner would raze a hotel to build a home, it is inconsistent with good husbandry and under the circumstances would be an unconscionable and unreasonable destruction of the inheritance. Thus, if A, fee simple owner of Blackacre, grants to B a life estate in the premises "without impeachment of waste," and Blackacre is a lot in a business district on which stands a six story hotel building, B would be enjoined if she threatened to raze the building and construct a single family dwelling thereon.

3. **Tenant's Tort Liability**

a. **Liability to Third Parties:** As discussed in the Torts Outline, a tenant, as occupier of the premises, may be liable in tort to third parties (e.g., licensees, invitees) for dangerous conditions or activities on the leased property.

C. LANDLORD DUTIES

1. **Duty to Deliver Possession of Premises**

a. **English Rule (Common Law View):** A landlord impliedly warrants that the tenant will have *a legal right to possession of the premises at the beginning of the term*.

b. **American Rule (Majority View):** Under the old American view, a landlord did *not* have an obligation to actually deliver possession to the tenant at the inception of the leasehold period. Consequently, a lessee did not acquire a legal interest in the leased premises until she actually took possession. In the event that there was a trespasser or holdover tenant on the property, the tenant's exclusive remedy was against the wrongdoer (and the tenant had no action against the landlord). *Note that, modernly, most states have statutes which require landlords to deliver possession to tenants at the beginning of the lease term*. Under this majority view, where the landlord does not deliver possession, he is in breach.

Question:

Hammer is the owner of a two-bedroom beachfront cottage in Rancho del Rio. In 1999 Hammer leased the dwelling to Sanchez with the occupancy period terminating on March 20, 2000.

On March 10, 2000, Hammer leased the Rancho Del Rio property to Farnsworth for six months. According to the written lease agreement, the tenancy would begin on April 1, 2000 and extend through September 30, 2000. On April 1st Sanchez is still in possession and refuses to vacate the premises despite the fact that his lease had expired. As a result, Farnsworth was prevented from taking possession.

Unable to take possession, Farnsworth refuses to pay Hammer the rent for the month of April. Hammer has instituted a suit against Farnsworth seeking to enforce their lease agreement and recover rent for the month of April. In accordance with relevant Anglo-Saxon case law, which party will most likely prevail?

(A) Hammer, because Farnsworth's only cause of action is against Sanchez, who is the holdover tenant.
(B) Hammer, because the landlord is under no obligation to deliver possession of the premises to the tenant.
(C) Farnsworth, because Hammer cannot deliver possession at the inception of the leasehold.
(D) There is a split of authority and the outcome will depend upon which rule of law is followed in this jurisdiction.

Answer:

(C) At common law, a landlord impliedly warrants that the tenant will have a legal right to possession of the premises at the beginning of the term. However, under the majority American view he does not have an obligation to actually deliver possession to the tenant. On the other hand, *under English law there is such an implied duty by the landlord to put the lessee in possession of the premises.* **Smith and Boyer, Survey of Property**, 2d. Ed., p. 138–140. It is agreed that the lease gives the tenant the legal right to possession, but the issue is whether the landlord impliedly agrees to enforce such right against a trespasser or a holdover tenant. All the cases agree that the tenant's exclusive remedy is against the wrongdoer and the tenant has no remedy against the landlord. Applying the majority American rule, Farnsworth's only cause of action would be the right to eject the tenant Sanchez, at sufferance, Choice (A) is incorrect, however, because *the question asks you to follow Anglo-Saxon case law*. Choice (C) is the best answer since Hammer failed to deliver possession of the premises to Farnsworth.

2. **Quiet Enjoyment:** In every lease there is an implied covenant of quiet enjoyment.

   a. **Eviction:** An eviction by the landlord breaches the covenant of quiet enjoyment and relieves the tenant of her obligation to pay rent.

      (1) **Actual Eviction:** Actual eviction occurs when the landlord or paramount title-holder excludes the tenant from the leased premises.

      (2) **Constructive Eviction:** As noted previously, a constructive eviction results from conduct or neglect by the landlord which makes the premises uninhabitable. To take advantage of this defense, the tenant must actually vacate the premises within a reasonable time. Once the tenant has vacated, he may cease paying rent.

3. **Premises Suitable for Particular Purpose:** A landlord generally does not impliedly warrant that the leased premises are suitable for any particular purpose, and she *is not liable for a dangerous condition existing on the leased premises*. Normally, the doctrine of "caveat emptor" prevails.

a. **Exceptions**

(1) **Dangerous condition at commencement of lease:** A landlord may be liable in tort to the tenant, her guests, licensees, and invitees, if at the commencement of the lease there is a dangerous condition which the landlord knows or should know about and the discovery of which would not likely occur by the tenant exercising due care.

(2) **Completely furnished dwelling:** A landlord in the lease of a completely furnished dwelling for a short period of time impliedly warrants the fitness of the premises and the furnishings. Thus, if injury results from defects therein, the landlord is liable.

4. **Duty to Repair**

a. **Common Law:** Under the common law and in the absence of a statute or covenant in the lease, the landlord is under *no duty to maintain the leased premises in a state of repair*. Modernly, of course, most leases do contain provisions requiring landlords to make repairs.

(1) **Negligent repair:** Although she may be under no duty to repair, if the landlord does undertake to repair and does so negligently, *she is liable in tort* for resulting injuries.

D. **TYPES OF LEASEHOLD ESTATES**

1. **Tenancies for a Term (or Tenancy for Years):** This type of tenancy has a fixed duration which is set forth in the lease, e.g., "for six months" or "for two years." It ends *automatically* at the expiration of the term unless the parties agree to renew it.

a. **Surrender:** A tenancy for years also terminates upon surrender (i.e., the tenant giving up her leasehold interest to the landlord and the landlord accepting).

2. **Periodic Tenancies:** A tenancy from period to period is a *continuing tenancy* and not the inception of a new tenancy at the beginning of each rental period.

a. **"Automatic Renewal":** This tenancy does not terminate at the end of any period but rather automatically renews for the next period (e.g., weekly or monthly) unless one of the parties gives timely notice of an intent to terminate at the end of the next period.

b. **Failure to Give Proper Notice:** There are usually statutory time periods (e.g., 30 days notice or a full period's notice) for the giving of notice to terminate a periodic tenancy. If the notice given is *not* in compliance with the statutory requirement, it is ineffective and the tenancy renews as if no notice had been given.

Example: A statute requires that all month-to-month tenancies be terminated by notice given not less than 30 days in advance of the date when the next period would begin. The landlord sends a notice on the 5th of May intended to terminate a month-to-month tenancy as of the 1st of June (the day when the next period begins). The notice is ineffective: the tenancy does not terminate on the 1st of June

(because notice was not given 30 days in advance). As a result, the tenant may remain in possession (though obligated to pay rent) until she receives a proper notice of termination.

3. **Tenancy at Will:** A tenancy at will is an estate in land that is terminable at the will of either the landlord or the tenant. At common law, this estate could be terminated by either party *without advance notice*.

    a. **Duration:** A tenancy at will continues until terminated by one of the parties. It can, however, be terminated by *operation of law* as where either party dies or the landlord leases property to another tenant.

    b. **Effect of Regular Rent Payments:** Note that a tenancy at will is quite rare. Unless the parties expressly agree that a tenancy will be a tenancy at will, where the tenant pays regular rent payments, the court will construe the tenancy to be a periodic tenancy.

    c. **Termination:** Because a tenancy at will may be terminated by either party without notice, tenancies at will are, as previously noted, quite rare. A tenancy at will may also terminate under several circumstances: (1) the death of either party; (2) where the tenant causes the premises to fall under disrepair such that the value of the property is affected; (3) where the tenant assigns his tenancy to someone else; (4) if the landlord leases the property to someone else; or (5) if the landlord conveys his interest in the property to a third person.

4. **Tenancies at Sufferance:** This type of tenancy arises *when a tenant wrongfully remains in possession after the expiration of a lawful tenancy (i.e. "holds over")*.

    a. **What Constitutes Holding Over?** A tenancy by sufferance arises when any tenant, for years, from year to year, month to month, or life tenant pur autre vie holds possession wrongfully beyond her term. *A holdover tenant differs from a trespasser only in that her original entry was rightful.*

    b. **Liability of Holdover Tenant:** Once the tenant at sufferance is removed from the land, then, by relation back to the beginning of her wrongful holding over, she is liable as though she were a trespasser from the date of the expiration of her lease, and judgment may be rendered against her for lost profits.

Question:

Marguarita entered into a three-year written lease for the rental of a dwelling house from Lawson, the landlord. The stipulated rent was $1,000 payable at the beginning of each month. The lease expired on May 31, 2001. Marguarita mistakenly believed that the lease terminated on June 30, 2001. On June 1, 2001 Marguarita sent a $1,000 rental payment to Lawson, which he accepted.

On June 20th Marguarita contacted Lawson and informed him that she would be vacating the premises at the end of the month. Lawson replied, "Sorry, you just obligated yourself to another term."

Marguarita refused to extend the lease beyond the month of June. Lawson brought an appropriate action against Marguarita to enforce an extension of the leasehold for a new term. If this jurisdiction follows common law rules on holdover tenancy, the court will likely rule in favor of

(A) Lawson, because his acceptance of the June rental payment created an affirmation of a new three-year tenancy
(B) Lawson, because a new one-year tenancy was created despite Marguarita's mistake
(C) Marguarita, because she was mistaken about the expiration date of the lease
(D) Marguarita, because her June rental payment created a month-to-month periodic tenancy, not the inception of a new three-year leasehold

Answer:

(B) Here's a rather puzzling Property question dealing with a unilateral mistake as it applies to a holdover tenant. In a lease for years no notice to quit is necessary on the part of either the landlord or the tenant. The term comes to an end at the expiration date with or without notice. When there is a holdover, the landlord at common law may do one of two things: (1) he may treat the tenant as a wrongdoer and proceed to eject him, or *(2) he may treat the tenant from period to period on the same terms as the prior lease. If the landlord chooses the second option, Smith and Boyer then point out "that the new tenancy is usually from year to year when the term of the original lease was one year or more."* **Real Property**, pg. 77. You may be "tempted" to choose (C), which admittedly is a very attractive answer choice. But it is necessary to remember that Marguarita's unilateral mistake will not provide a valid defense. It is well established that a unilateral mistake will not prevent formation of a contract unless the non-mistaken party knows or should know of the other's mistake. Since the facts don't indicate that Lawson was aware of Marguarita's mistake, she will be bound for a year-to-year tenancy. Even though it may be a harsh decision to swallow, remember that these Property questions are based upon strict and inflexible English common law principles.

   c. **Landlord Remedies:** If a tenant continues in possession after his right to possession has ended, the landlord may (1) evict him or (2) bind him over to a new periodic tenancy. At common law, the new tenancy was usually from year to year when the term of the original lease was one year or more. However, under the modern view most states today regard the new tenancy as running from month to month.

E. ASSIGNMENTS AND SUBLEASES

1. In General

Absent an express provision in the lease prohibiting or restricting transfers, a tenant may freely transfer her leasehold interest in whole or part. If she makes a complete transfer of *her entire remaining estate,* she has made an *assignment*; conversely, where *she retains any part* of her leasehold interest, then the transfer is a *sublease*.

2. **Assignment:** If the transfer effectuates an assignment, the assignee stands in the shoes of the original tenant. Remember that in order to create an assignment, the original tenant must transfer the entire remaining estate. In other words, for example, where a tenant has a three-year lease, and she transfers possession after one year, she must transfer the entire remaining two years in order to create a valid assignment.

3. **Effect of Assignment**

   a. **The Tenant:** The duty of a tenant to perform those obligations for which she covenanted in her lease *is not ended* when she assigns away her leasehold. Although the original tenant is no longer in privity of estate with the landlord, there is still *privity of contract*. Thus, if the assignee fails to make the rental payments, the landlord can recover against the tenant.

   b. **The Assignee:** Assignees are bound to perform the original covenants in the lease if they either "assume" them or if the covenants "run with the land" (e.g., covenant to pay rent or covenant to pay taxes on leased premises). When assignees assume covenants they, in effect, make the same promise to the landlord as did the original tenant.

      (1) **Privity of Estate and Contract Between Landlord and Assignee:** There is privity of estate between the landlord and assignee. Moreover, if the assignee assumes the duties under the lease, then privity of contract exists as well.

Question:

Bing owned a ten-story apartment building in Syracuse. Bing entered into a one year written lease with Camby with the tenancy period running from January 1st to December 31st. The stipulated monthly rental was $2,000. At the end of September (the ninth month of the lease), Camby assigned the premises to Delp. At that point in time, Camby had made the rental payments for the first nine months of the leasehold. Delp took possession on October 1st and made the rental payment for that month to Bing.

Delp did not pay the rent for November and vacated the premises on November 30th. The premises remained unoccupied for December and no rental payment was made for that month.

Thereafter Bing sued Camby and Delp for the non-payment of rent. The court should rule that

(A) Camby is liable for $2,000 and Delp is liable for $2,000
(B) Camby and Delp are jointly and severally liable for $4,000
(C) Delp is liable for $4,000
(D Delp is liable for $2,000 and Camby is liable for $4,000

Answer:

(B) An assignment arises where a lessee transfers the entire leasehold balance to an assignee. The assignee is then in privity of estate with the lessor and is primarily liable for payment of rent. In addition, the lessee-assignor remains in privity of

contract with the lessor and is secondarily liable for payment of rent, similar to that of a surety. Smith and Boyer, **Survey of Property**, pg. 147. In this question Camby assigned his leasehold to Delp. Both parties are jointly and severally liable to Bing for the $4,000 rent for November and December. Delp is primarily liable and Camby is secondarily liable. Bing may recover the $4,000 from either party. Choice (B) is correct. Note that if Bing recovers from Camby, Camby would, in turn, be subrogated to Bing's rights against Delp, who as assignee, is primarily liable for the rent payment.

4. **Effect of a Second Assignment**

   a. **Privity of Estate with Landlord Ends:** If the assignee reassigns the leasehold interest, her privity of estate with the landlord ends. Thus, assignees who have ***not assumed*** have no further liability for any of the covenants of the lease once they make a further assignment of their interest. However, if the first assignee specifically promised the landlord that she would pay rent (or "assumed other obligations") then there would be liability based on ***privity of contract***.

5. **Effect of a Sublease:** A sublease is created when a tenant transfers less than the entire remaining term of the lease. For example, where a tenant has a three-year lease, and, after one year, transfers possession of the premises for one year, she has created a sublease.

   a. **The Tenant:** The tenant-sublessor remains both in privity of estate and in privity of contract with the landlord and thus continues to be obligated to pay the rent.

   b. **The Sublessee:** A sublease creates no legal relationship between the landlord and the subtenant. In other words, the tenant remains the landlord's tenant, and the subtenant in effect becomes the tenant of the original tenant. As a result, the sublessee is ***not liable to the landlord to pay rent*** (or any other covenants in the lease). This is because there is neither privity of estate nor privity of contract between the sublessee and the landlord.

6. **Assignment by the Landlord**

   a. **In General:** The landlord's reversionary interest is also assignable; the sale of an occupied apartment building, for example, constitutes such a transfer. Upon completion of the assignment, all burdens and benefits formerly cast upon the landlord are now transferred to the assignee (e.g., the right to receive rents). Note, however, that where the original landlord made covenants to the tenant, he still remains liable for these covenants. Recognition of the new landlord by the tenants is called ***attornment***.

7. **Covenants Against Assignment or Sublease**

   a. **Strictly Construed Against Landlord:** Many leases contain covenants on the part of the tenant not to assign or sublease without the consent of the landlord. These are strictly construed against the landlord. Thus, a covenant prohibiting assignments does not prohibit subleasing and vice versa.

      (1) **Waiver:** Although a lease may contain a valid covenant prohibiting assignments, the covenant may be waived if the landlord knows of the tenant's

assignment and does not object (e.g., the landlord accepts rent from the assignee).

F. FIXTURES

A fixture is a chattel that has become real property. An article of personal property may become a fixture (a) without any physical attachment to the land other than the fact that it rests thereon of its own weight (e.g., a prefabricated house is moved onto Blackacre and is set on a pre-constructed cement foundation); or (b) by being set in and annexed to the soil itself (e.g., a fence post placed in a hole in the ground); or (c) by being on the land (e.g., a house is already an accession to or a fixture on Blackacre and a pre-constructed window frame is fitted and attached to the house or a table is built in a room of the house).

1. **Intention of the Annexer:** Whether or not a particular article is a fixture is primarily a question of the intention of the annexer. This is an objective intention that is inferred by taking into account the following considerations:

   a. The nature of the article;

   b. The manner of annexation to the land;

   c. The injury to the land, if any, by its removal;

   d. The completeness with which the chattel is integrated with the use to which the land is being put;

   e. The relation which the annexer has with the land such as licensee, tenant at will for years, or fee owner; and

   f. The relation that the annexer has with the chattel such as owner, bailee, or converter.

2. **Requirements:** For a chattel to become a fixture, three essential elements must concur:

   a. ***The chattel must be annexed to the realty either actually or constructively*** (e.g., an engine which is bolted to the cement floor of a building is actually annexed to the land but a wheelbarrow used on a farm is neither actually nor constructively annexed to the land).

   b. ***The chattel must be appropriated to the purpose for which the land is used*** (e.g., an air compressor used to hoist automobiles for greasing purposes in a gasoline station is appropriated to the purpose for which the land is used).

   c. ***It must be the intention of the annexer that the chattel become a fixture***.

3. **Trade Fixtures:** These are chattels annexed to the land by a tenant for pecuniary gain during her tenancy. They are removable by the tenant, whether she be a tenant for life, tenant for years, or tenant at will.

a. **Common Law Rule:** If the tenancy is for a definite time and ends on a certain day, the trade fixtures must be removed ***before*** the end of the term (e.g., L leases Blackacre to T as a store for three years. The term expires December 31, 2003. T during the term firmly affixes shelves to the floor of the store building. T does not remove them before midnight of December 31, 2003. The shelves remain fixtures on the property and belong to landlord L).

b. **Modern View:** Most states refuse to follow the common law rule that a tenant forfeits his trade fixtures by failing to remove them before expiration of the lease term. To encourage trade and industry ***a tenant is permitted to remove trade fixtures within a reasonable time after the expiration of a lease***.

Question:

Hardcastle leased a 7,500 square foot store from Llewelyn, the landlord, for a period of five years. Planning to open a hardware business, Hardcastle renovated the interior. He hired a contractor who installed overhead lighting and built wooden shelves that were nailed into the walls. The contractor also constructed free-standing tables for displaying merchandise. In addition, Hardcastle hired a builder who constructed a second floor balcony that was structurally attached to the main building. The balcony gave Hardcastle additional store footage to sell more items and expand his business potential.

At the expiration of the lease, Hardcastle decided to vacate the premises and remove the improvements which he made. He began disassembling the balcony and started removing the lighting, shelving and free standing tables. Llewelyn immediately filed suit seeking to enjoin Hardcastle from removing these items.

The court will most likely allow Hardcastle to remove

(A) everything
(B) everything except the balcony
(C) everything except the balcony and the shelves
(D) the free-standing tables only

Answer:

(B) Questions involving trade fixtures frequently appear on the bar exam. ***Trade*** fixtures are ***chattels annexed to the land by a tenant for pecuniary gain during his*** tenancy. ***As a general rule, trade fixtures are removable by the tenant unless*** accession occurs. Regarding the doctrine of accession, Smith and Boyer provide an example where a steel "I" beam is built into a structure. The beam thus becomes an accession to the property. As such, it loses its identity as a trade fixture and is not removable. **Real Property**, pg. 226. By analogy, the balcony, which is structurally attached to the main building, is viewed as an accession. Choice (B) is therefore correct as all other chattels are trade fixtures and removable.

4. **Common Ownership Cases:** Where both the chattel and the land are owned by the annexor, common consequences are:

   a. **Subsequent Sale:** A deed to the real property will transfer all of the fixtures as well. Thus a deed describing the lot also transfers the house on the lot and also transfers the plumbing fixtures in the house.

   b. **Death:** At common law, realty descended to the heir, whereas personalty passed to the next of kin. In such a case, the fixtures go with the realty.

   c. **Mortgage:** A mortgage on the property will cover all fixtures including, generally, those subsequently affixed.

      (1) **Lien on chattel affixed to real property – UCC Rule:** Under UCC § 9-313(4), where a mortgagor purchases a chattel and affixes it to the real property, it becomes part of the real property, but, where there is a lien on the chattel, the seller of the chattel also retains a security interest in the chattel. Under this section of the UCC, where the seller of the chattel retains a purchase money security interest, this interest trumps even a mortgage that was recorded prior to the lien, so long as the seller of the chattel records his interest within ten days after the mortgagor affixes the chattel to the land. This recordation is called a *"fixture filing."*

      Example: Maggie Mortgagor purchases a water softener from Sam Shopowner on credit. Maggie grants Sam a security interest in the water softener. The water softener will be subject to UCC § 9-313(4), and therefore Sam must record his security interest in the water softener. If he records the lien, he will succeed in a post-default action over the mortgagee of Maggie's land.

      (2) **Common law rule:** Under the common law, where a mortgagor attaches a chattel to the real property that has been purchased on credit, the lien holder will win if he records his interest first, and the mortgagor will win if his interest is recorded first. Therefore, under the common law, the classic race to record applies.

   d. **Taxation:** Fixtures are taxed as real rather than as personal property.

   e. **Eminent Domain:** When the real property is condemned, the condemnor must pay for the fixtures (whereas personalty need not be paid for and is to be instead removed by the owner).

5. **Divided Ownership Cases:** Where the chattel and the land are owned by different persons (e.g., a landlord and a tenant), the following rules apply:

   a. **Tenants:** When a tenant affixes personalty to the premises, and these chattels are deemed to be subject to the balancing fixtures test described *supra*, they become part of the realty and title passes to the landlord. Removal by the tenant thereafter would be waste.

      (1) **Trade fixture exception:** A tenant is allowed to remove fixtures installed for the purpose of trade on or before termination of the lease (see *supra*). In some

states, the trade fixture exception has been broadened to include domestic and/or ornamental fixtures.

(2) **Duty to repair damages caused by removal:** Tenants are responsible for repairing damages caused by removal of "trade fixtures."

b. **Trespasser/Adverse Possessor:** Trespassers and adverse possessors (who make annexations before the running of the statute of limitations) lose title to the improvements if they constitute fixtures.

(1) **Rationale:** In accordance with the "intention test," a good faith trespasser, who believes land to be her own, normally intends the annexation to be permanent.

III. RIGHTS INCIDENT TO POSSESSION AND OWNERSHIP OF LAND

A. ADVERSE POSSESSION

1. **Application of Statute of Limitations**

The doctrine of adverse possession is based on statutes of limitation for recovery of real property. Statutes of limitation operate not only to bar one's right to recover real property held adversely by another for a specified period of time, but also to vest the disseisor (i.e., the adverse possessor) with a perfect title as if there had been a conveyance by deed. The concept behind adverse possession is that where the title owner of the property has notice of someone else's claim to the property and does not bring an action to eject such person from the premises within the statutory period, he waives his right to do so, and title should be transferred to the "trespasser."

2. **Requirements**

In order to hold real property adversely, one's possession must be:

a. *Actual and Exclusive* (meaning sole physical occupancy),

b. *Hostile and Adverse* (meaning not permissive),

c. *Open and Notorious* (meaning not secret or clandestine but occupying as an owner would occupy, for the whole world to see),

d. *Continuous* (meaning without interruption for the statutory period, whether it be 5, 7, 10, 15, or 20 years), and

e. *Peaceable* (meaning no physical eviction or eviction by court action).

3. **Prescriptive Period Defined by Statute**

Each jurisdiction has an adverse possession statute defining the period for which a trespasser must actually occupy the land. The statute of limitations under the prescriptive period statute begins to run when the trespasser enters onto the record titleholder's property and begins to possess it. At this point in time, should the record titleholder

wish to, he could bring suit to eject the trespasser/claimant. As long as the landlord brings suit before the Statute of Limitations has run, he will be entitled to reclaim his property, even if judgment is rendered after the prescriptive period has run out.

4. **Burden of Proof**

   All the elements noted above must co-exist. Needless to say, to take real property away from its owner by adverse possession is a very drastic procedure. As a result, the adverse possessor bears the burden of proof to show the elements exist by a preponderance *of the evidence*.

5. **Limitation of Adverse Possessor's Claims**

   a. **Adverse Possessor Cannot Acquire a Larger Estate than Claimed**

      No adverse possessor can acquire by her adverse possession a larger estate in the land than that which she has claimed throughout the entire period of her adverse possession. For example, if X has claimed only a life estate by adverse possession, she can mature title only to a life estate.

   b. **Adverse Possessor Cannot Claim Title to Less Than a Freehold Estate**

      No one claiming less than a freehold estate in land can obtain title through adverse possession. This means that the adverse possessor must claim either a (1) life estate, (2) a fee tail, or (3) a fee simple.

      Rationale: This is so because only one claiming a freehold estate can be seized.

6. **Recording**

   The recording statutes have no application to title by adverse possession. Some states, however, do require the recording of the instrument upon which the claim is based in order to satisfy the requirements of adverse possession under color of title.

7. **Tacking**

   There need not be continuous possession by the same person. The period of adverse possession of one possessor can be tacked to the period of adverse possession of another possessor *when there is privity between the two*.

   a. **Privity**

      Privity exists when the possession is passed from one to another by deed, will, descent, written contract, oral contract, mere oral permission, or consent.

      Note: Tacking is *not* permitted where one adverse claimant ousts a preceding adverse claimant.

8. **Disability**

   One who is under a disability (e.g., minority, imprisonment, or insanity) at the time of the accrual of the cause of action against the adverse possessor is given, by statute, time beyond the removal of his disability in which to bring his action.

a. **No Tacking of Disabilities**

Only a disability of the *owner* existing at the time the cause of action arose is considered. Thus, disabilities of successors in interest or subsequent additional disabilities of the owner have no effect on the statute.

b. **Multiple Disabilities**

If two or more disabilities exist in the original owner at the time the cause of action accrues, the owner may take advantage of the disability that lasts the longest.

Question:

In 1950, Jason Woodstock owned Twin Oaks, a forty-acre tract outside of White Plains in Yorkshire County. The following year, Jason devised Twin Oaks "to my son, Socrates, and my daughter, Delilah, for their respective lives as tenants in common, then to the heirs of my son." Jason died in 1952. On January 1, 1953, Sampson went in to adverse possession of Twin Oaks. On July 1, 1962, Socrates died leaving Homer as his only heir. Homer was exactly nine years old at Socrates' death.

Two weeks after her brother's death, Delilah committed suicide. Sampson has been in continuous possession of Twin Oaks since January 1, 1953. The period of majority in this jurisdiction is 21 years of age. The Statute of Limitation on adverse possession in this jurisdiction is 20 years. In addition, this jurisdiction has the following statute in effect:

"An action for the recovery of land shall be commenced only within twenty years after the right of action first occurred, but if a person entitled to bring such action, at the time the cause therof occurs, is within the age of minority, of unsound mind, or imprisoned, such person after the expiration of twenty years from the time the cause of action occurs, may bring such action within ten years after such disability is removed."

On July 1, 1975, Homer brought an action for ejectment against Sampson. Judgment for

(A) Homer, even though he was not a life in being at the time of the devise in 1951
(B) Homer, since his minority tolled Sampson's period of adverse possession
(C) Sampson, since he acquired a fee simple interest to Twin Oaks by adverse possession
(D) Sampson, only if his possession of Twin Oaks was open, hostile, and notorious

Answer:

(B) At the time of the commencement of Sampson's adverse possession, Socrates and Delilah had life estates while Homer had a vested remainder in fee simple. When Sampson took possession of the premises, he trespassed on the possession of

Socrates and Delilah, not on the possession of Homer. Indeed, Homer had no right to possess Twin Oaks until the death of the life tenants. Hence, Homer had no cause of action against Sampson and no statutory period began to run against Homer. When Socrates and Delilah died in 1962, Homer was 9 years of age. Based on the tolling statute in effect, Homer is given an additional ten years after the disability is removed to bring his cause of action against Sampson.

9. **Land that Is Not Subject to Adverse Possession**

Land that is owned by the government is not subject to adverse possession. Similarly, land registered under a Torrens System is not subject to adverse possession.

MULTISTATE CHART:

ADVERSE POSSESSION

INTENT	The adverse claimant must intend to claim the land as his own.
STATUTORY PERIOD	Possession must be for the statutory period.
OPEN AND NOTORIOUS	The occupation must be open and notorious.
ACTUAL POSSESSION	The adverse claimant must be in actual possession of the land.
CONTINUOUS	The possession must be continuous throughout the statutory period.

B. **LATERAL AND SUBJACENT SUPPORT**

1. **Right to Lateral Support**

The right of a landowner to have his land supported laterally by the neighboring land is an absolute right inherent in the land itself and a part thereof.

a. **Support of Land in its Natural Condition:** The right of lateral support means the land in its *natural condition* without any buildings or other artificial structures. One who by excavation or otherwise withdraws lateral support from his neighbor's land is *absolutely and strictly liable* (regardless of negligence).

b. **Support of Land with Artificial Structures:** If there are artificial structures on the land and the land in its natural condition would be injured by the taking away of lateral support, then there are two distinct views as to the damages recoverable:

(1) **English rule:** In a minority of jurisdictions, the recovery will include both the damage to the land *and* the damage to the artificial structures thereon as well.

(2) **American rule:** In most states, the *recovery is limited to damage to the land in its natural condition* and does not include any damage to the artificial structures on the land.

(3) **Negligent excavation:** Under both the English and American rules, however, if there is *negligence* on the part of the wrongdoer who removes lateral or

subjacent support, then the wrongdoer is liable for all damages which naturally and proximately flow from his negligence, including damages to both land and artificial structures.

Question:

The following incident occurred during the heavy rains that battered Southern California in the winter and spring of 1995. On February 12, 1995, a violent storm struck the Los Angeles basin area. Triggered by heavy rains and wind gusts of over 50 mph, a mudslide caused Velma Vogel's house to be swept downhill into a home owned by Marilyn Malibu. After the Vogel home crashed into Malibu's, the mudslide then carried both of them into the ocean.

Undisputed evidence revealed that the mudslide started when a large plot of land, situated on an uphill slope, owned by the Seabreeze Realty Co., slid downward across Pacific Coast Highway towards the ocean. The landslide then caused the Vogel dwelling to dislodge, rotate and press against the home of her neighbor, Marilyn Malibu, and both homes then slid into the sea.

Malibu asserts a claim against Vogel to recover damages to her home caused by the mudslide. Judgment for whom?

(A) Malibu, because a landowner has the absolute right to have his land supported laterally by the neighboring land
(B) Malibu, because one who withdraws lateral support from his neighbor's land is liable for the injury done to such land in its natural condition, regardless of negligence
(C) Vogel, because although Malibu may recover for injury to the land in its natural condition, she cannot recover for injury to the artificial structures thereon
(D) Vogel, because Malibu's proper cause of action should be against Seabreeze Realty Co.

Answer:

(C) If there are artificial structures on the land and the land in its natural condition would be injured by the taking away of lateral support, then there are two distinct views as to the damages recoverable: (a) in some states the recovery will include both the damages to the land and the damage to the artificial structures thereon (called the English rule), (b) *but in the majority of states the recovery is limited to damage to the land in its natural condition and may not include any damage to the artificial structures on the land (called the American rule)*. The theory of the American rule is that to permit the wronged landowner to recover for damage to his buildings is in substance a requirement that the adjoining landowner's land furnish lateral support for both the land and the buildings of the plaintiff.

2. **Right to Subjacent Support**

The right to subjacent support means support from underneath the surface of the land as distinguished from the sides and the rights involved are substantially the same as

those involved in lateral support. This right usually arises when the owner of the land has granted the right to mine on his land to a third party.

a. **Natural and Artificial Conditions:** Unlike with lateral support, a landowner has an absolute right to subjacent support for land in its natural state and also for any artificial structures on the land that existed when the right to mine was granted.

b. **Interference with Underground Waters:** If one excavates on his land and such excavation releases *semi-fluid* or *semi-solid material* from under his neighbor's land causing the neighbor's land to sink, there is liability. However, an adjoining landowner is *not liable* for interfering with underground percolating waters.

C. WATER RIGHTS

1. **In General:** Title to lands under *non-navigable* streams is in the abutting owner and extends to the center of the stream. The same holds true in the case of lakes. A stream or lake is considered navigable if it can be used for commerce. The title to lands under *navigable streams or lakes* is usually in the state through which the stream flows or in which the lake is located.

2. **Classification of Waters**

   a. **Lakes and Streams on the Surface**

   b. **Underground or Percolating Waters**

   c. **Surface Waters.**

3. **Water Rights Relating to Lakes and Streams**

   a. **Riparian Rights:** Under this doctrine that is predominant in approximately 33 states, all tracts of land which abut or touch the water of a lake or stream are riparian. To be a riparian, one needs only to be an owner of riparian land. No one can be a riparian who does not own riparian land. Riparian lands are lands within the watershed.

      (1) **Natural flow theory:** Each proprietor of land on a stream or lake has a fundamental right to have the stream or lake remain substantially in its natural state, *free from any unreasonable diminution in quantity and free from any unreasonable pollution in quality*. Each riparian may use the water for either natural or artificial wants so long as he uses it only on riparian land and does not sensibly affect the quantity or quality of the water.

         (a) **Rights of lower riparian owners:** A lower riparian has a right of action against an upper riparian whenever the latter's use of the water materially affects either the quantity or quality of the lake or stream waters, even though such use results in no injury or damage to the lower riparian.

         (b) **Benefit:** This theory has the merit of being relatively certain and definite so that the riparian owner knows fairly well just how far he can go in his use of the water.

(2) **Reasonable Use Theory:** Each riparian proprietor has the fundamental right to make the *maximum use* of the water in the stream or lake *provided such use does not unreasonably interfere* with the like use by other riparians. Each riparian may use the water for any beneficial use either on riparian or nonriparian lands so long as the use does not interfere with the reasonable use by other riparians. Reasonable use alone constitutes the measure and limit of the water right.

   (a) **Rights of lower riparian owners:** A lower riparian has no right of action against an upper riparian until he can show that the use is unreasonable.

   (b) **Benefit:** This theory has the merit of giving each riparian the right to make the *maximum beneficial use* of the water available, but its weakness is its indefiniteness, for no riparian can determine the extent of his rights as against his fellow riparians.

b. **Natural vs. Artificial Use:** Under both theories, water uses are designated as either "natural" or "artificial." The former include(s) uses necessary for the daily sustenance of human beings (namely, household consumption, gardening, etc.). Conversely, artificial uses consist of irrigation, power, mining, manufacturing, and industry.

   (1) **Majority view:** The use of water for *natural purposes is paramount and takes precedence* over the use of water for artificial purposes. Thus, although upper riparians can take all the water they need for natural uses, they cannot take for artificial purposes unless there is enough water for the domestic needs of the lower riparians.

c. **Prior Appropriation Doctrine:** This system is the sole basis of water rights in the eight states of Arizona, Colorado, Idaho, Nevada, New Mexico, Utah, Wyoming, Montana, and nine other states west of the Mississippi River. It is sometimes called the "Rocky Mountain" view. The distinguishing feature of this doctrine is "first in time is first in right"; there is no equality of rights and no reasonable use.

   (1) **Requirements:**

      (a) Intent to appropriate water,

      (b) Divert the water from the source of supply, and

      (c) Beneficial use of such water.

Question:

Carson is the owner of a parcel of land known as Tall Acres which is situated upon the top of Candy Rock Mountain. Located below Tall Acres is Grasslands, a forty-acre hillside estate which is owned by DuVall. Crystal Stream is a nonnavigable watercourse that originates at the top of Candy Rock Mountain and runs all the way down into the San Vicente Valley. Both Tall Acres and Grasslands are within the watershed of Crystal Stream.

When DuVall purchased Grasslands in 1956, he started taking water from Crystal Stream and used it to irrigate the southern half of his property which he has used as a farm. Prior to 1956, the southern half of Grasslands had been cleared and placed in cultivation, while the northern half remained wooded and unused except for an occasional hike or gathering of timber for use as domestic fuel. DuVall continued this established pattern of use. Now (January, 1992), he is still taking water from Crystal Stream and using it to irrigate the southern half of Grasslands.

In 1990, Carson built a home on Tall Acres and started taking water from Crystal Stream for domestic purposes. During that year there was heavy rainfall, and this caused Crystal Stream to run down the mountain at a high water level. The next year, however, there was a drought. As a result, Crystal Stream flowed at a very low level. Consequently, there was only enough water to irrigate DuVall's farmland or, in the alternative, to supply all of Carson's domestic water needs and one quarter of DuVall's irrigation requirements. Candy Rock Mountain is located in a jurisdiction where the period of prescription is fifteen years.

Inasmuch as Crystal Stream is still flowing at a very low level and Carson is continuing to take water for his personal needs, there is insufficient water to irrigate Grasslands. As a consequence, DuVall brings an appropriate action to declare that his water rights to the stream are superior to those of Carson. In addition DuVall moves to have the full flow of Crystal Stream passed to him, notwithstanding the effect it might have on Carson.

If this state follows the doctrine of prior appropriation, judgment for whom?

(A) Carson, because as an upstream landowner, he would have superior rights to the water over a downstream owner
(B) Carson, because domestic use is superior to and is protected against an agricultural use
(C) DuVall, because he has obtained an easement by prescription to remove as much water as he may need
(D) DuVall, because he has put the water to a beneficial use prior to Carson's use and has continuously used the water

Answer:

(D) According to the prior appropriation doctrine, "first in time is first in right." In contradiction, under the riparian rights doctrine the use of water for natural purposes is paramount and takes precedence over use of water for artificial purposes.

MULTISTATE CHART

RIPARIAN DOCTRINE	PRIOR APPROPRIATION DOCTRINE
1. THE DISTINGUISHING FEATURE OF THE RIPARIAN DOCTRINE IS EQUALITY OF RIGHTS AND REASONABLE USE – there is no priority of rights; the reasonable use by each is limited by a like reasonable use in every other riparian.	1. THE DISTINGUISHING FEATURE OF THE PRIOR APPROPRIATION DOCTRINE IS FIRST IN TIME IS FIRST IN RIGHT – there is no equality of rights and no reasonable use limited by the rights of others
2. To be a riparian one needs only to be an owner of riparian land. Riparian land is land which abuts or touches the water of a lake or stream.	2. To be a prior appropriator one must do three things: (a) have an intent to appropriate water, (b) divert the water from the source of supply, and (c) put such water to a beneficial use.
3. Riparian lands are lands within the watershed. Under the natural flow theory a riparian cannot use water on non-riparian lands, that is, beyond the watershed from which the water cannot return to the stream from which it is taken. Under the reasonable use theory a riparian may use water on non-riparian lands if such use is reasonable.	3. The prior appropriator may use the appropriated water on riparian and on nonriparian lands alike. The character of the land is quite immaterial.
4. Under the riparian doctrine the use of water for *natural* purposes is paramount and takes precedence over the use of water for *artificial* purposes. Natural uses include domestic purposes for the household and drink, stock watering, and irrigating the garden. Artificial purposes include use of irrigation, power, mining, manufacturing, and industry.	4. The prior appropriation doctrine makes no distinction between uses of water for natural wants and for artificial and industrial purposes.

4. **Water Rights Relating to Underground or Percolating Waters**

   a. **Common Law Rule:** Percolating water under the surface is subject to the ***absolute control and ownership*** of the surface owner, and if the withdrawal affects the neighboring landowner, it is ***damnun absque injuria*** for which there is no legal redress.

   b. **The "Reasonable Use" Doctrine (American Rule):** In a majority of states, the owner of the surface may withdraw the percolating water from underneath the land and make ***reasonable use*** thereof. Using such water beneficially on his land or to develop such land is reasonable even though it injures his neighboring landowner. But using such percolating water on land other than that from which

it is withdrawn or using it as an article of merchandise elsewhere is unreasonable when such use injures the neighboring proprietor.

5. **Water Rights Relating to Surface Waters**

a. **Common Law ("Common Enemy") Rule:** In a majority of states, a landowner has *unlimited discretion* in dealing with surface waters (e.g., floods, melting, snow, rainfall) regardless of the effect on others. In theory, surface water is viewed as a "common enemy" and any owner can build dikes or change drainage to get rid of it.

b. **Civil Law Rule:** Each landowner has a right to the *natural flow* of surface waters and a corresponding duty not to interfere with such natural flow, thus in effect imposing a servitude on the lower tract owner to receive and carry off surface waters from the higher tract. Under this rule, a landowner may not divert surface waters onto neighboring lands if in so doing he would damage them.

c. **The "Reasonable Use" Rule:** A small number of states require that the landowner's conduct be reasonable in the light of all relevant circumstances, including the benefit to himself and the harm which results to others (i.e., a balancing test).

D. **EMBLEMENTS**

Absent severance, property ownership includes surface rights, rights with respect to the area below the surface (subterranean rights), and rights with respect to the area above the surface (air rights). Surface rights may include natural vegetation (i.e., trees, shrubs, etc.), growing crops, and chattels attached to the land (fixtures).

1. **Fructus Naturales**

Trees, grasses, and perennial shrubs *(fructus naturales)* are considered a part of the land. If the trunks or roots are located on the property line of adjoining landowners, the landowners own the trees as tenants in common.

a. **Fructus Naturales** will pass with a conveyance of the land. They are also included within the scope of a mortgage of the land unless specifically reserved by contract.

b. **The Statute of Frauds** applies to the sale of fructus naturales. The sale of fructus naturales is considered a sale of an interest in land subject to recordation unless immediate severance is to be made by the vendee or by the vendor.

c. **Real Property:** *According to the prevailing view, fructus naturales are and remain real property until they are actually severed from the land.*

2. **Fructus Industriales and the Doctrine of Emblements**

a. **Definition:** *Fructus industriales or emblements are annual growing crops* resulting from the cultivation and labor of man. *These growing crops are usually classified as personal property.*

b. **Scope:** Growing crops are included within the scope of a sale or mortgage of the land unless expressly excepted.

c. **Contract:** A contract of sale for growing crops is treated as a contract to sell the crops when they come into existence.

d. **Personal Property:** Growing crops are subject to administration **as personal property** if the landowner dies intestate. Growing crops are considered part of the land and pass to the devisee of the land if the landowner dies testate but makes no specific gift of the emblements.

Question:

A deed executed by A in 2005 conveyed Blackacre for a consideration of one dollar, receipt of which was acknowledged, "to B for life, but if liquor is ever sold on Blackacre, then to C and his heirs, and if for any reason the interest hereby conveyed to C is not valid, then I reserve the right to reenter Blackacre and take back my property." In 2007, B died before the wheat he had planted could be harvested.

Who is entitled to the proceeds of the crops?

(A) B's heirs
(B) C
(C) A
(D) The crops should be divided equally between B's heirs and A.

Answer:

(A) For Multistate purposes, you are required to know that there are two types of crops: (1) *fructus naturales*—crops which come from nature's bounty without the aid of man, such as trees, bushes, grasses and their fruits, and (2) *fructus industriales*—crops which come primarily from man's annual planting, cultivating, and fertilizing, such as wheat, beans, corn, and citrus fruits in orchards. According to the prevailing view, *fructus naturales* are and remain real property for all purposes until they are actually severed from the land. On the other hand, *fructus industriales* (also referred to as emblements) are annual crops which are for most purposes personal property. See Smith and Boyer, **Law of Property,** pp. 244-245. Since wheat is a *fructus industriales* crop (or an emblement), it is viewed as being personalty, and therefore the proceeds from its sale pass to the life tenant's heirs. Consequently, choice (A) is correct.

3. **Doctrine of Emblements**

A tenant has an irrevocable license to care for and harvest crops planted during his tenancy, if his tenancy was for an uncertain term and the tenancy was not terminated because of the tenant's acts. The tenant is entitled to the harvest following his tenancy and is not entitled to subsequent harvests from regenerative crops. A life tenant's estate retains the right to harvest the crops planted in the year of the tenant's death absent express language to the contrary in the granting deed or will.

IV. NON-POSSESSORY INTERESTS IN LAND

A. EASEMENTS AND PROFITS

1. Profit-a-Prendre Defined

A profit is the right of one person to go onto the land in possession of another and take therefrom either some part of the land itself or some product of the land. For example, A has the right to enter Blackacre which is in the possession of B, and take off oil, gravel, marble, stone or grass, trees, shrubbery, or fish.

   a. **Easement vs. Profit:** The distinguishing element between an easement and a profit is that while an easement gives its owner only the right to enter or use the land of another (with no right to take anything from such land), a profit on the other hand gives its owner the right to take either the soil itself or some product of the land.

   b. **Interest in Land:** A profit is an interest in land and requires compliance with the Statute of Frauds.

   c. **Non-possessory:** A profit is a non-possessory interest in land. It should be distinguished from the possessory interest in owning the soil or minerals beneath the surface.

   Caveat: A right to come onto property and take water is an easement, whereas a right to come onto property and take ice is a profit because ice is considered a product of the soil. Since water is owned by no one but belongs to everyone, it is not considered as connected with any particular piece of land and is not considered a product of the soil. Thus, the right to take water from the land of another is treated merely as a right to use the land and therefore only an easement.

Question:

   Woody, a famous environmentalist in the State of Sylvania, was the owner of Pocono Woods, a large tract of virgin forest. In 1995, Woody conveyed Pocono Woods "to the people of the State of Sylvania in fee simple, provided, however, that if any portion of said tract shall ever be used or developed for any commercial purpose or otherwise converted from its natural state (with the exception for recreational, scientific, or educational purposes), then the grantor or his successors in interest may reenter as of the grantor's former estate."

Under Sylvania law, conveyances of real property to "the people" of the State are deemed to vest title in the State regarded as a legal entity, and custody over such property resides in an appointed official known as the Director of Environmental Resources. In 2005, the Director granted Crockett Company the privilege to cut timber on a remote portion of Pocono Woods, together with incidental easements of way. The section that Crockett Company was to clear would be used for the development of a state recreation area.

After the privilege was granted, Crockett proceeded to clear the timber which he later sold for $10,000.00. When Woody learned that Crockett was cutting the timber and selling it, he notified the Director to desist further exploitation of the land.

The right of Crockett to cut and sell the timber which was to be cleared from Pocono Woods would be an example of a(an)

(A) license
(B) easement appurtenant
(C) easement in gross
(D) profit-a-prendre

Answer:

(D) A *profit-a-prendre* is similar to an easement in that it is a non-possessory interest. The holder of the profit is entitled to enter upon the servient tenement and take the substance of the land *(e.g.,* minerals, trees, oil, or game) subject to the privilege. In this regard, a profit, like an easement, may be appurtenant or in gross.

2. **Easements**

    a. **Definition:** An easement is the right of one person to go onto the land in possession of another and make a limited use thereof. For example, A has a right to enter or walk across Blackacre which is in the possession of B.

    b. **Classification:** Easements (or profits) are classified as follows:

       (1) *easements appurtenant* and

       (2) *easements in gross.*

    c. **Easement Appurtenant:** An easement (or profit) is appurtenant when it is attached to a piece of land and benefits the owner of such land in his use and enjoyment thereof. Every easement appurtenant requires two pieces of land which are owned by two different persons. For example, A is the owner in fee simple of Blackacre, a five-acre tract, on which he maintains a dwelling house for himself and family. Abutting Blackacre is Whiteacre, which is owned by B. By deed, A grants to B and his heirs a right of way across a strip of land along the north edge of Blackacre. B thus has an easement appurtenant across Blackacre.

(1) The two pieces of land involved in an easement appurtenant are

   (a) **the dominant tenement**, which is the land whose owner is benefited by the easement. In the example above, Whiteacre is the dominant tenement; and

   (b) **the servient tenement**, which is the land whose owner is burdened by (or subject to) the easement, and is Blackacre in the example given above.

(2) The owner of the dominant tenement is called the ***dominant tenant***; whereas the owner of the servient tenement is called the ***servient tenant***.

(3) **Easements appurtenant run with the land**; in other words, where the land is transferred, the easement appurtenant will transfer to the new owner of the land.

d. **Easement in Gross:** An easement (or profit) is in gross when it is intended to benefit the owner or possessor personally rather than in connection with any land the holder owns. In other words, every easement in gross requires only one piece of land (i.e., the servient tenement) which is owned by a person other than the owner of the easement in gross. There is no dominant tenement. The servient tenement is the land subject to and burdened by the easement. For example, A conveys "to B Utility Company and its assigns the right to install electrical wires along the north edge of Blackacre." B Utility Company, which does not own any land adjacent to Blackacre, has an easement in gross across the servient tenement (i.e., Blackacre). The owner of the easement in gross is called the dominant tenant (even though no dominant tenement exists).

Question:

On October 1, 1920, Jackson Stone, owner of several hundred acres in the County of Los Angeles, drafted a general development plan for the area, to be known as the Del Mar addition. The duly recorded plan imposed elaborate limitations and restrictions upon the land in the addition, which was to be developed as a residential district. The restrictions were to extend to all persons acquiring any of the lots and to their heirs, assigns, and lessees. It was further provided that all subsequent owners would be charged with due notice of the restrictions.

Among those restrictions in the general plan were the following:

   (22) A franchise right is created in a strip of land ten feet in width along the rear of each lot for the use of public utility companies with right of ingress and egress.

   (23) No house or structure of any kind shall be built on the aforementioned strip of land running through the said blocks.

In 1940, Heather Anne purchased one of the lots, built a house, and erected a fence at the rear of her property within the restricted area. In 1944, Wilber Hemmings purchased a lot adjacent to the Anne property and built a new house. Two years later, Sam Roberts purchased the lot which adjoined Wilber's property.

The three deeds to these properties each contained reference to the deed-book where the general plan was recorded.

In 1948, Sam Roberts began the construction of a seven-foot post and rail fence along the line dividing his lot with Wilber's and along the center of the area subject to the franchise right. Although Wilber objected to its construction, the fence was completed.

The franchise right created for the public utility companies would most likely be an example of a(an)

(A) license
(B) equitable servitude
(C) easement appurtenant
(D) easement in gross

Answer:

(D) The franchise right would be construed as an easement in gross. This non-possessory interest is created when the holder of the easement interest acquires his right of special use in the servient tenement independent of his ownership or possession of another tract of land. In an easement in gross, the easement holder is not benefited in his use and enjoyment of a possessory estate (*i.e.,* there is no dominant tenement) by virtue of the acquisition of that privilege. Choice (B) is incorrect since an equitable servitude is a restriction on the use of the owner's land. Alternative (A) is incorrect since a license is a revocable privilege to enter upon the land of another. Choice (C) is wrong because the utility company did not possess an adjoining dominant tenement.

e. **Affirmative vs. Negative Easements**

(1) **Affirmative easements**

Affirmative easements entitle the easement holder or owner to make ***affirmative use*** of the servient tenement (e.g., laying and maintaining sewer lines, draining water, or simply having a right-of-way). In other words, the dominant tenement owner is privileged to make affirmative use of the servient tenement.

(2) **Negative easements**

Negative easements ***prevent*** the servient tenement owner from doing some act or making a particular use of her own land. For example, B, the owner of Blackacre which is located between the ocean and A's Whiteacre, agrees in writing that no structure will be built on Blackacre that will interfere with A's view of the ocean. A thus has a negative easement on Blackacre, the servient tenement that bears the burden of a negative easement. **Note:** Keep in mind that a negative easement is negative in another sense: it does not permit the dominant tenant to engage in any affirmative act on the servient tenement.

MBE tip: Negative easements for light, air, and view have been repudiated in most jurisdictions. For purposes of the MBE, where you see a plaintiff bringing an action against a defendant for a right to a view, or sunlight, or fresh air, you should assume that such a right probably does not exist and that the plaintiff's claim will probably be unsuccessful.

f. Creation

(1) Creation by writing

An easement (or profit) is an interest in land and therefore requires compliance with the Statute of Frauds in the creation or transfer thereof. As a general rule, the writing or express grant must be signed by the party to be bound (or the initial holder of the servient tenement).

(2) Creation by implication

An easement may also be created, though not expressly in a writing, by implication. An easement by implication generally arises when the owner of two or more adjacent parcels sells one or more of them and it is clear (although no easement was mentioned in the instrument of conveyance) that one was intended. In order to establish an easement by implication, the following requirements must be met:

(a) that at the time of the conveyance one part of the land is being used for the benefit of the other part (a quasi-easement); *and*

(b) that the use is apparent; *and*

(c) that the use is continuous; *and*

(d) that the use is either *reasonably or strictly necessary* to the enjoyment of the quasi-dominant tract.

(3) Easements implied by grant and reservation

If the implied easement is in favor of the conveyee and is appurtenant to the tract conveyed, it is called an *implied grant*. On the other hand, if the implied easement is in favor of the conveyor and is appurtenant to the tract retained, it is called an *implied reservation*.

g. Creation of Easements

(1) Easements (or profits) may thus be created as follows:

(a) **by express provision in a deed or will;**

(b) **by implication:** this arises from the circumstances surrounding the dividing by the owner of a piece of land into two pieces and conveying one of such pieces to another. Easements by implication include: (a) *easements of necessity* and (b) easements created by conveyances in reference to a plat depicting streets, parks, and other places thereon;

(c) **by prescription**: this arises by adverse use of the servient tenement by the dominant tenant for the period of the statute of limitations (or prescriptive period). To mature such an easement, the use must be (as with adverse possession) (a) adverse as distinct from permissive, (b) open and notorious, (c) continuous and without interruption, and (d) for the statutory period;

(d) **by estoppel**; and

(e) **by eminent domain**.

h. **Extinguishment**

The instrument creating an easement (or profit) may expressly state the terms on which the interest is to expire (e.g., at the end of a specified number of years). If expiration is not specified in the instrument, the easement (or profit) is considered to be ongoing. However, they may be terminated in a number of different ways:

(1) **Release**

The holder of the benefit of an easement or profit (i.e., the dominant tenant) may execute a release, thereby terminating the burden of the servient tenement. Such a release must be in writing and comply with the Statute of Frauds.

(2) **Merger**

When the fee simple title to both the servient and dominant estates comes into the hands of a single person, merger extinguishes the easement. The rationale is that one cannot have an easement in his own property. **Note:** Termination of an easement by merger applies only to an easement appurtenant.

Question:

Rose, owner of Roseacre, granted to Morgan, owner of Diamondacre, an easement of way. Rose then went to Japan to live. Morgan then moved into possession of Roseacre and used it openly and exclusively, paying the taxes, for 23 years. He did not use his easement during that period. Rose returned and tried to evict Morgan from Roseacre. The court held that Morgan had acquired Roseacre by adverse possession. Morgan then sold Roseacre back to Rose, who then put a chain across the easement. Morgan brought an action to remove the chain.

In most jurisdictions, Morgan will

(A) lose, because he abandoned his easement
(B) lose, because he did not use his easement for the statutory period of 20 years
(C) lose, because rather than using his easement, he used all of Roseacre
(D) win, because mere non-use of an easement does not extinguish it

Answer:

(C) This is an example of the extinguishment of an easement by merger. An easement appurtenant is terminated by merger when the dominant and servient tenements come into common ownership. Choice (A) is incorrect because failure to use an easement or profit will not result in extinguishment. Note, however, that non-use coupled with physical acts which clearly indicate the user's intent to abandon may be sufficient to effectuate an extinguishment. As a general review, remember that an easement or a profit may be terminated in one of the following ways: (1) by merger, (2) by written release, (3) by non-use coupled with acts which indicate an intent to abandon, (4) by prescription, (5) by destruction of the servient tenement, or (6) by estoppel.

(3) Condemnation

Condemnation of the servient estate will extinguish the nonpossessory interest. According to the modern view, the holder of the benefit is entitled to compensation for the value lost.

(4) Abandonment

A clear showing by the dominant tenant that he ***intends to abandon the use*** (and evidenced by his conduct) will extinguish an easement.

(a) Non-use

Non-use of an easement, no matter how long continued, will ***not*** be sufficient to terminate an easement. However, non-use ***coupled with an intent to abandon*** is sufficient to constitute an abandonment. Remember that an intent to abandon must be evidenced by conduct.

Example: North Shore Railway Company is granted an easement across Black Acre. The easement is to lay railroad tracks and run trains. If North Shore Railway Company stops running trains, it has stopped using its easement. Such conduct alone does not constitute abandonment. However, if North Shore Railway picks up the track, this conduct will evidence an intent to abandon and will constitute abandonment.

(b) Excessive use

Excessive use of an easement does not forfeit or extinguish the easement. In such case, the servient tenant may enjoin the dominant tenant's excessive use of the easement, but the dominant tenant may still use the easement within the scope or extent thereof as created.

(5) Destruction of the servient tenement

If the easement is in a structure (e.g., a staircase or hallway), involuntary destruction of the structure (e.g., by fire or flood) will extinguish the easement.

(6) Prescription

When the servient tenant has used her land continuously and uninterruptedly for the statutory period of prescription in a way inconsistent with and adverse to the easement and without consent of the dominant tenant, then the easement is extinguished by prescription.

(7) Estoppel

When the servient tenant, in reasonable reliance on conduct of the dominant tenant, uses his servient tenement in a manner inconsistent with the existence of the easement and it would be inequitable to pen-nit further use of the easement, such easement is extinguished by estoppel.

B. LICENSES

1. **Definition:** A license simply ***permits one person to come onto the land in the possession of another without being a trespasser***. Unlike an affirmative easement, a license is not an interest in land. It is merely a privilege, revocable at the will of the licensor (unless it is coupled with an interest).

Question:

The Miami Marlins is a professional baseball team that plays its home games at the Fish Bowl. Ricardo Renteria purchased season tickets to the Marlins baseball games. Ricardo was an avid fan who attended every home game. At the start of the season, Hugh Zinger, the Marlins' owner, traded away all the top players on the team. Consequently, the Marlins performed pitifully and began losing practically every game.

Ricardo became disgusted with the Marlins and blamed Zinger for the team's lousy performance. In protest, Ricardo began wearing a placard at the Fish Bowl which read, "BOYCOTT THE MARLINS . . . ZING ZINGER." During the games Ricardo would march around the stadium with his placard and begin chanting: "Zinger sucks . . . Zinger sucks."

As the season progressed, the fans became disgruntled and joined Ricardo in his protests. Soon thereafter, Ricardo received a notice from the Marlins' management revoking his season tickets. Ricardo was informed that he would not be allowed to attend any more Marlins games, but would receive full reimbursement for all remaining games.

If Ricardo brings an appropriate action against the Marlins challenging the revocation of his season tickets, he will

(A) win, because he was entitled to express his rights of free speech
(B) win, because he had paid for the tickets for the whole season
(C) lose, because his license to attend games was revocable
(D) lose, because obscene speech is not constitutionally protected

Answer:

(C) According to Smith and Boyer, *ticket holders to baseball games, horse races, polo, hockey contests, and other entertainment spectacles have only a mere license which is always revocable*. A license simply permits one person to come onto land in the possession of another without being a trespasser. Since a license is revocable, choice (C) is correct. There is a minority view which holds that a ticket holder has a contract with the stadium owner. In such situations, the contract right is specifically enforceable and the ticket holder has a right to use self help in remaining on the land. However, this is the minority view and, thus, choice (B) is not the best answer.

2. **Classifications**

   a. **A License or Mere License,** which is always revocable

   b. **A License Coupled with an Interest,** which is irrevocable

   c. **An Executed License** (i.e., an oral license acted upon), which is irrevocable

3. **Compare with Lease:** A license may be distinguished from a lease since a licensee never has possession of land. A lessee, on the other hand, always has possession of the land.

4. **Compare with Easement:** An easement is a substantial incorporeal interest in the land of another and is created in most cases by a deed of conveyance. It is an interest in land and requires for its creation a compliance with the Statute of Frauds. On the other hand, a mere license is no such interest in land and requires no formalities for its creation.

5. **Compare with a Contract:** A contract is always based on a consideration theory. There may or may not be a consideration for a license. For example, if A permits B to come onto A's land to park his car for two hours with no consideration involved, then B has a mere license. This license is revocable at any time by A. Note, however, the following variation: A permits B to come onto A's property to park his car for two hours and B pays A $2.00 for A's agreement that B may do so without interruption. B has a license to park on A's property, which is revocable, but he also has a contract under which A has promised for a consideration not to revoke the license. Although A has the right and power to revoke the license, he has only the power but no right to breach the contract (and A is liable if he does so).

C. COVENANTS RUNNING WITH THE LAND

1. **Legal Effect: Contracts**

   It may prove helpful in our understanding of covenants running with the land to first review the legal effect of contracts and easements. As a general rule, a contract operates to bind person to person. Thus only the promisor is bound to perform the promise and only the promisee has a right to compel performance of the promisor. Note the following exceptions: (a) the case in which a third person (e.g., intended third-party beneficiary) for whose benefit a contract is made; (b) the case in which the promisee assigns the benefit of the contract to an assignee who may, without being party

to the contract, enforce it against the promisor; and (c) covenants running with the land which one may, without being a party to the contract, enforce simply by virtue of becoming owner of the estate in the land.

2. **Legal Effect: Easements**

Whereas the legal effect of a contract is to bind person to person, an easement appurtenant (or profit) operates to bind land to land. The dominant tenant owns "an interest in the land of another." If A transfers her dominant tenement to B, the benefit of the easement (or profit) appurtenant passes to the conveyee. By the same token, a transfer of the servient estate carries with it the burden of the easement (or profit) appurtenant. The successor in interest to either estate must recognize the easement (or profit) as an interest in the land.

3. **Legal Effect: Covenants Running with the Land**

A covenant running with the land is something of a hybrid between a contract and an easement. It is more than just a personal contract and less than an easement (or profit) in the sense that a covenant is not "an interest in land." Rather, a covenant running with the land is attached or connected with the estate since it may be enforced against, or by, someone who is not one of the original parties to the covenant, solely by virtue of having succeeded to the ownership of the property to which the covenant referred.

4. **Types of Covenants**

   a. **Affirmative Covenant**

   An affirmative covenant will bind the covenantee or the holder of the servient estate to do some affirmative act.

   b. **Negative Covenant**

   A negative covenant will prohibit the holder of the servient tenement from doing something with respect to the land.

5. **Requirements**

   a. **Covenant**

   There must be a covenant or writing that is signed and complies with the Statute of Frauds.

   b. **Intention**

   It must be the intent of the covenantor and covenantee that the covenant run with the land. As long as the words *assigns* or *successors* are used in the instrument, the intention is usually clear that the covenant is intended to run.

   c. **"Touch and Concern" the Land**

   The covenant must be of a type that ***touches and concerns the land***. This simply means that the effect of the covenant is to make the land either more valuable

(or increase its utility) in the hands of the covenantee or less valuable (or curtail the use or utility of the land) in the hands of the covenantor. In other words, the benefit of the covenant usually touches and concerns the land of the covenantee, while the burden touches and concerns the land of the covenantor.

Note: The reverse is also true. In either case, however, the covenant must affect the legal relations of the parties as *landowners* and not as members of the community at large.

d. **Privity of Estate**

There must be privity of estate between the original covenanting parties. Although there are divergent views as to what relationships satisfy this requirement, privity of estate (for MBE purposes) usually means that *one of the contracting parties succeeds to an interest in the land of the other party* (e.g., landlord-tenant or grantor-grantee).

6. **Types of Covenants Running with the Land**

a. **To Pay Rent**

b. **To Insure the Buildings on Leased Premises**

c. **To Pay Taxes on the Leased Premises**

REQUIREMENTS FOR THE RUNNING OF COVENANTS

	AT LAW				IN EQUITY			
	Affirmative		Negative		Affirmative		Negative	
	Benefit	Burden	Benefit	Burden	Benefit	Burden	Benefit	Burden
Horizontal Privity	No	Yes	No	Yes	Generally not enforced by the Courts. If a Court does enforce an Affirmative Covenant, the Requirements for a Negative Servitude Apply.		No	No
Vertical Privity	Yes	Yes	Yes	Yes			No	No
Notice to person being charged	No	Yes	No	Yes			No, generally presumed	No, generally presumed
Intent for covenant to run	Yes	Yes	Yes	Yes			Yes, generally implied by a common plan or scheme	Yes
Touch and Concern the land	Benefit	Burden (Restatement requires Benefit, too)	Benefit	Burden (Restatement requires Benefit, too)			Attenuated Benefit	Attenuated Burden (Restatement requires Benefit, too)

KAPLAN *pmbr*

d. **Option to Purchase Leased Premises**

e. **Not to Sell Intoxicating Liquor on Leased Premises**

f. **To Build a Structure on Leased Premises**

g. **Not to Assign or Sublease Premises**

h. **To Supply Water, Light, or Heat on Leased Premises**

7. **Types of Covenants That Do Not Run with the Land**

a. **Not to Compete in Business**

b. **To Pay Promissory Note of the Covenantee**

c. **To Pay Taxes on Land Other than Leased Premises**

d. **Purely Personal Covenants**

8. **Enforceability**

As a general rule, covenants running with the land are enforceable in ***actions at law*** (e.g., breach of contract or breach of covenant). In this case, the breaching party is liable for money damages. Note, however, that in certain cases (where the remedy at law is inadequate) the plaintiff can proceed in ***equity*** (e.g., injunctive relief).

9. **Termination**

Basically, the same rules governing the extinguishment of easements (and profits) are also applicable to covenants, including merger, abandonment, and estoppel. Note, however, that when the covenant is one enforceable by many persons (e.g., in a common development or subdivision scheme), release by the original covenantee (i.e., the subdivider) will ***not*** affect the rights of the others in the subdivision to enforce it against the party who received the release.

10. **Remedies**

The remedy for violation of a covenant will generally be money damages.

D. **EQUITABLE SERVITUDES**

1. **Definition**

An equitable servitude is a restriction on the use of land enforceable in a court of equity. An equitable servitude is more than a covenant running with the land because it is "an interest in land." It is important to note that an equitable servitude is broader than an "equitable easement" because it applies not only to land but also to chattel property, such as a business.

2. **Requirements**

   a. **Writing**

   An equitable servitude may be created by any writing complying with the Statute of Frauds evincing an intention that such servitude exist.

   b. **Intention**

   The intention of the parties determines who may and who may not enforce an equitable servitude. No particular words are essential to the creation of an equitable servitude provided an *intention to bind the land* and not merely the persons to the transaction can be found from the instrument and the circumstances surrounding its execution.

   c. **Notice**

   The transferee must take the land with either actual or constructive notice of the existence of the servitude. On the other hand, an equitable servitude *cannot be enforced* against a person who gives value and has *no notice* of the existence of the servitude (namely, a bona fide purchaser).

   d. **Privity Not Required**

   Unlike in a covenant, privity is not required for equitable servitude because the servitude is considered to be an equitable property interest in the land and not a right of the owner of the servient tenement.

3. **Enforceability**

An equitable servitude may be enforced against one of the parties or her transferee with notice, as to land acquired after the creation of the original relationship between the parties. **Caveat:** A court of equity *may refuse to enforce* an equitable servitude in the following situations:

   a. If its purpose is contrary to public policy;

   b. When the granting of relief would do more harm than good;

   c. When the granting of the relief prayed for would be futile; or

   d. The plaintiff is guilty of laches, or unclean hands (i.e., the person seeking enforcement is guilty of a similar violation).

4. **Common Development Schemes**

When a landowner owns a large parcel of land and subsequently divides it into smaller parcels for purposes of development (e.g., a subdivision), that landowner may place restrictions in the deed of the parcels. Occasionally, the landowner will place the restrictions in the deed of some parcels, but not in all. Under the *"collateral document rule,"* where the developer intends a common scheme for the entire parcel of land, including all of the plots, a land owner whose deed does not contain the restriction may be bound by the restriction if the other deeds of the adjacent properties contain the restriction.

a. **Common Scheme Required:** The collateral document rule only applies where the original landowner intended for all of the plots to be bound by the restriction.

b. **Notice Required:** The purchaser of a plot whose deed does not contain the restriction is deemed to be on constructive notice of the contents of the deeds of adjacent properties. This notice is, of course, constructive notice. However, the purchaser of a plot does not have to be on actual notice of the restriction to be bound by it.

5. **Extinguishment**

As a general rule, equitable servitudes may be extinguished in the same way as easements and profits. This includes release, merger, abandonment, and so on.

a. **Changed Neighborhood Conditions**

Changed neighborhood conditions may also operate to terminate an equitable servitude. For example, if a subdivision is restricted to residential purposes only and the neighborhood has so changed (e.g., commercial development) that the purpose of the restrictions can no longer be accomplished, then the servitude is extinguished.

b. **Zoning:** According to the prevailing view, equitable servitudes are not invalidated by zoning ordinances that are inconsistent with the private restrictions unless neighborhood conditions have changed sufficiently to make the servitude meaningless.

6. **Remedies**

The remedy for violation of an equitable servitude will generally be specific performance or an injunction.

MULTISTATE NUANCE CHART:

COVENANT RUNNING WITH THE LAND	EQUITABLE SERVITUDE
1. Is more than a mere personal contract but is less than an easement because technically it is **not** an "interest in land."	1. Is a restriction on the use of the land enforceable in a court of equity.
2. **Requirements:** (a) there must be a covenant, (b) an intention that the covenant run with the land, (c) must "touch and concern" the land, and (d) privity of estate.	2. Is more than a covenant running with the land, because it is an interest in land.
3. A covenant "touches and concerns" the land if it makes the land in the hands of the owner either more usable and more valuable or less usable and less valuable.	3. Is broader than an equitable easement because it applies not only to land but also to chattel property, such as a business.
4. **Legal effect:** is to make an assignee of the land either benefit by or be burdened by the covenant without being party to the making of the contract.	4. **Requirements:** (a) may be created by a writing complying with the Statute of Frauds, (b) intention of the parties that there be a restriction, and (c) transferee takes the land with either actual or constructive notice of the existence of the servitude.
5. **Remedies for breach:** standard contract remedies (i.e., money damages or specific performance if appropriate).	5. Privity of estate is **not** required.
	6. **Remedies:** equitable remedies.
	7. Extinguished: (a) by doing an act which violates the servitude and continuing for the period of the statute of limitations, (b) release by the dominant tenant, or (c) where the purpose and object of the servitude become impossible to achieve (e.g., change in character of neighborhood from residential to commercial).

V. LAND USE CONTROL

A. ZONING

1. Zoning Power

A state's enabling act is the source of state and local zoning powers. All city and county zoning ordinances must conform to and be authorized by the state legislature.

2. Zoning Theory

a. Segregation by Uses

Zoning laws may be used to segregate incompatible uses from developing in the same area.

(1) Single family residences are normally considered the highest and best use in zoning ordinances.

(2) Commercial and industrial uses are lower uses and generally incompatible with residential neighborhoods.

(3) Cumulative use zoning allows for a higher use, such as a single-family residence, to be built on land zoned for a lower use, such as apartment house zoning.

(4) Noncumulative zoning prohibits any use, other than the zoned use, from being built on the zoned lot.

b. Density Control Zoning

(1) Height limitations are used to regulate high-rise development.

(2) Setback requirements are normally tied to the height limitation requiring a certain amount of setback from the street based on the height of the building.

3. Constitutional Issues

a. **Police Power Authority:** States enact zoning legislation *under their police power authority*. Zoning ordinances are presumed constitutionally valid.

b. **Due Process:** Procedural due process may be violated if a zoning ordinance is enacted without notice and an opportunity to be heard afforded to the affected landowners.

c. **Equal Protection Clause:** The Equal Protection Clause requires that similarly situated landowners be treated similarly.

(1) The *"rational basis" test* (rational relationship to a legitimate state interest) is usually applied to Equal Protection claims.

(2) The *"strict scrutiny" test* (where the state must show a compelling state interest) is applied to a zoning ordinance that operates against a suspect class or violates a fundamental interest.

d. **Fifth Amendment:** The 5th Amendment prohibits the state from taking property *without just compensation*. A zoning ordinance is void if it violates the 5th Amendment.

B. EMINENT DOMAIN

1. **Taking: Definition:** A taking occurs when the government takes title to land, physically invades the land, or severely restricts the use of land.

2. **Protective Regulation:** A regulation that has the purpose or effect of protecting the public from harm is considered a valid exercise of the state's police power and non-compensable.

3. **Public Benefit:** A regulation that has the purpose or effect of extracting a public benefit at the expense of the landowner is considered an exercise of eminent domain, and the landowner is entitled to just compensation. A balancing test is applied to balance the landowner's loss against the public's interest.

4. **Partial Taking Damages:** A landowner is entitled to recover damages for the harm to his remaining property in the case of a partial taking.

VI. CONVEYANCING

A. HISTORICAL OVERVIEW

1. **Conveyances at Common Law**

   Feoffment involved a symbolic delivery of land by livery of seisin and was the important common law method of conveying a freehold estate. Other transfer methods included exchange, partition, fine and common recovery, lease and release, surrender, and dedication.

2. **Conveyances Under the Statute of Uses**

   The *Statute of Uses*, passed in 1536, made conveying a freehold estate possible without the livery of seisin ceremony. Title could pass through a bargain and sale transaction or by a covenant to stand seized.

3. **Conveyances in the United States**

   Statutes usually provide that freehold estates may be conveyed by deed and other methods recognized at common law or under the Statute of Uses. A writing that evidences an intention to convey an estate will be sustained as a conveyance despite informal language.

B. CONVEYANCING BY DEED

1. **Essential Formalities in the Execution of a Deed**

   The Statute of Frauds requires a written instrument signed by the grantor or the grantor's agent to accomplish the conveyance of a freehold estate, the execution of a contract for the sale of land, or a memorandum of sale. An oral contract for the sale

of land may be specifically enforceable in equity under the part performance doctrine (see the following).

a. **Seal:** A seal is not necessary in connection with a conveyance of a possessory estate in a majority of the states.

b. **Signature of Grantor:** The signature of the grantor is usually required by statute for the proper execution of a deed. The grantee's signature is not required. The grantee's acceptance of the instrument makes him a party to the deed.

c. **Acknowledgment:** Attestation and acknowledgment are not usually required for the due execution of the deed. Statutes often require acknowledgment as a prerequisite to recordation.

d. **Consideration:** Consideration is necessary to raise a use (under the Statute of Uses) by bargain and sale. The recital of a consideration in the instrument will suffice. A conveyance will be sustained if consideration was paid but no recital was included in the deed.

e. **Identification of the Parties:** In order for a deed to be valid, both the buyer and the seller must be identified in the deed. A person to whom a deed is delivered may have the authority to fill in the name of the grantee if a bona fide purchaser or mortgagee is involved.

f. **Description of the Property:** A deed must adequately describe the property being conveyed.

2. **The Doctrine of Part Performance**

In a majority of states, ***an oral real estate sales agreement may be enforced in equity*** (even though the Statute of Frauds requires a writing). Although there is considerable flexibility among the states as to the kind and amount of part performance that is necessary in order to permit enforcement, the following acts are generally necessary:

a. *Payment of all or part of the purchase price, and either*

b. *Delivery of possession of the land or premises to the vendee, or*

c. *Construction of permanent and valuable improvements by the vendee.*

3. **Delivery of Deeds**

An ***effective delivery*** of a deed requires that the ***grantor intend to deliver the deed***. A physical transfer of the deed is not necessary. A presumption of delivery arises when the grantee possesses the deed or when the grantor records the transfer. Once a deed has been delivered, a cancellation of the instrument will not revest ownership of the property in the grantor.

a. **Power to Recall:** A grantor may properly retain the power to revoke a conveyed estate. There is no delivery when the grantor retains a power to recall the deed at any time.

b. **Delivery: Estoppel:** A grantor may be estopped to deny the fact of delivery if he prepares a proper deed, and the grantee acquires possession of the property and creates rights in a **bona fide** purchaser or mortgagee.

c. **Third Party:** A grantor may deliver a deed to a third party with instructions to deliver the deed to the grantee after the grantor's death.

d. **Escrow:** An escrow involves the deposit of a properly executed deed by the grantor with a third party who is to deliver the deed to the grantor upon the happening or performance of a named event.

 (1) **Custodian vs. agent:** At the outset, the third party is a mere custodian of the escrow property. After substantial performance of the stated conditions, the third party becomes an agent of the grantee with respect to the deed and an agent of the grantor with respect to the consideration.

 (2) **Ownership transfer:** Ownership passes to the escrow grantee upon the happening or performance of the named conditions or events without a physical transfer of the deed to the grantee. Absent estoppel, an escrow grantee that obtains wrongful possession of the deed cannot create rights in a third party that are superior to those of the escrow grantor.

 (3) **Timing:** The passing of title to the escrow grantee relates back to the date of the inception of the escrow. This fiction is applied to adjust the equities of the parties.

 (4) **Conditions:** If the deed is delivered directly to the grantee, he acquires ownership free from any conditions not specifically included in the deed. Extrinsic evidence is admissible to distinguish a condition precedent from a condition subsequent.

4. **Acceptance by the Grantee**

Acceptance by the grantee is required for a conveyance by deed. At common law, acceptance was presumed if the conveyance was beneficial to the grantee.

5. **Description of Land**

A description is sufficient if the land can be identified from the description in the contract or deed. Where a description is insufficient, title does not pass to the grantee. A description **may be incorporated by reference** and it may be based on a private or government survey.

a. **Part of a Larger Tract:** The conveyance of a part of a larger tract, rather than an undivided interest, must include a description sufficient to identify the area involved.

b. **Conflicts:** If a description contains conflicting or ambiguous measurements, priority is given to the description concerning which the parties are least likely to be mistaken.

c. **Measurement:** Title passes to the center of a monument if the grantor is the owner of that area. Actual measurement of the area conveyed is made from the side of the monument.

d. **Good Lead:** If a deed contains a "good lead," or sufficient description so that the grantee can ascertain the meaning of the deed, the description will be sufficient. For example, if the grantor conveys "all my land," the deed need not contain a description of that land.

e. **Parole Evidence:** If a description needs supplementation, or if it is ambiguous, parole evidence will be admissible to clear up the ambiguity.

f. **Rules of Construction:** Occasionally, there is an inconsistency or a mistake in the description of the land being conveyed. In this case, rules of construction are generally followed unless clear and convincing evidence demonstrates an attempt to the contrary. (1) Natural monuments (*e.g.*, trees) trump any other descriptive terms (other types of descriptions, courses and distances, and artificial monuments); (2) artificial monuments (*e.g.*, buildings, streets, statues) defeat all other descriptions except for natural monuments; (3) courses (*i.e.*, angles) trump descriptions of distances or directions (*e.g.*, "east 120 degrees to Maple Avenue" trumps "east 500 feet to Maple Avenue"); and (4) general descriptions are least useful.

g. **Reformation:** Where a deed does not represent the intent of the parties, reformation is an available remedy. Reformation is available when there is a typographical error or when the parties were mutually mistaken as to the terms of the land sale agreement. Where there has been a unilateral mistake, reformation is only appropriate if the non-mistaken party misrepresented a material term. Note that where a bona fide purchaser relies on the language of the original deed, reformation is not an available remedy.

Question:

Rockne Faust owned Scenicacre, a 40-acre tract of farmland, which was located in the township of South Bend. Rockne leased the property and building thereon to Dan Devine for a term of seven years commencing on February 15, 1970 and terminating at 12 noon on February 15, 1977. The lease contained the following provision: "Lessee covenants to pay the rent of $1000.00 per month on the fifteenth day of each month and to keep the building situated upon said leased premises in as good repair as it was at the time of said lease until the expiration thereof." The lease also contained a provision giving Devine the option to purchase 10 acres of Scenicacre for $30,000.00 at the expiration of the lease term. Before the lease was executed, Faust orally promised Devine that he (Faust) would have the 10-acre tract surveyed.

During the last year of the lease, Devine decided to exercise the option to purchase 10 acres of Scenicacre. Without Faust's knowledge, Devine began to build an irrigation ditch across the northern section of the property. When Devine notified Faust that he planned to exercise the option, Faust refused to perform. Faust also informed Devine that he never had the 10-acre tract surveyed.

If Devine brings suit for specific performance, which of the following is Faust's best defense?

(A) The option agreement was unenforceable under the parole evidence rule.
(B) Faust's failure to survey the 10-acre tract excused him from further obligations under the contract.
(C) The description of the property was too indefinite to permit the remedy sought.
(D) The option was unenforceable because it lacked separate consideration.

Answer:

(C) Smith and Boyer note that no conveyance is valid unless the description of the land sought to be conveyed is sufficient to identify the land. Scenicacre is a 40 acre tract of farmland in this example. The leasehold agreement provided that Devine would have an option to purchase 10 acres of Scenicacre at the end of the lease term. Since the lease failed to identify or describe a distinct piece of Scenicacre, Faust's best argument is that the option should fail for lack of a definite description.

6. Equitable Conversion

The doctrine of equitable conversion treats interests in land as if the land had already been converted into personal property. Equitable conversion is based on the maxim that equity regards as done that which ought to be done. Most states follow the doctrine of equitable conversion.

a. Application

Equitable conversion applies when there is an enforceable obligation to sell land (usually in the case of an executory real estate sales contract). Under this doctrine, the *purchaser is regarded as the equitable owner of the land*, and the *vendor, although she still owns the legal title, is regarded as the beneficial (or equitable) owner of personal property*, primarily the right to the purchase price. This means that where real property under contract is destroyed during the executory period and before the closing, and neither party is at fault, the risk of loss is on the buyer. In other words, even if the property is completely destroyed, under the doctrine of equitable conversion, the buyer must pay the contract price.

Question:

On July 1, Vendor and Vendee entered into a written real estate sales agreement in which Vendor agreed to sell Greenview, a 100 acre parcel, to Vendee for the purchase price of $500,000. The sales agreement stipulated that closing was set for September 15 "or anytime before."

On August 1, the state government instituted a condemnation suit on the Greenview property. The state Department of Transportation planned to construct a new highway over Greenview. On September 1, the condemnation was finalized

and Vendor received $550,000 from the state government for the "taking" or acquisition of Greenview. When Vendee learned of the condemnation, he contacted Vendor and claimed that she was entitled to a share of the condemnation award. Vendor thereupon deposited $500,000 in his own personal bank account and deposited $50,000 into an escrow account pending resolution of the dispute.

Is Vendee entitled to share in the condemnation award?

(A) Yes, because Vendee owned equitable title to the property based upon the doctrine of equitable conversion.

(B) Yes, because under the terms of the sales agreement Vendee had the legal right to close before the date of condemnation.

(C) No, because Vendor owned legal title to the property at the time of the condemnation.

(D) No, because the risk of loss was on the Vendee.

Answer:

(A) Under equitable conversion the purchaser is regarded as the "equitable" owner of the land although legal title remains with the seller. In the absence of a contract provision to the contrary, ***the weight of authority applies the equitable conversion doctrine and shifts the risk of loss to the vendee for casualty losses which occur during the existence of the vendor-vendee relationship***. By the same token, ***the doctrine also "shifts the benefits to the purchaser as well."*** **Real Estate Transactions**, Burke, pg. 45. With regard to the shifting of benefits, Burke points out that if minerals are discovered on the property during the executory period, the person bearing the risk of loss should in fairness also receive the benefits of the appreciation in value. In like manner, since the property appreciated in value during the executory period as a result of the condemnation, Vendee will be entitled to the appreciation in value. Therefore, choice (A) is correct.

(1) **Minority rules**

(a) **Uniform Vendor and Purchaser Risk Act ("UVPRA")**: Under the Uniform Vendor and Purchaser Risk Act, the risk of loss remains on the seller during the executory period (until the closing) unless the buyer has actually taken possession or holds legal title to the property at the time the property is destroyed. About thirteen states follow the UVPRA.

(b) **Uniform Land Transactions Act ("ULTA")**: Under the Uniform Land Transactions Act, which has not yet been enacted by any legislature, risk of loss also remains on the seller until the buyer either takes possession or holds legal title.

(c) **Application of UVPRA and ULTA**: Both model statutes require the seller to allow the buyer to cancel the contract during the executory period if a material loss occurs.

b. **Vendor's Death**

When the vendor dies during the existence of a specifically enforceable contract, the beneficial interest descends as personal property and the heir gets only a bare legal title, which she must convey to the purchaser when the purchaser performs.

c. **Purchaser's Death**

When the purchaser dies during the existence of an enforceable contract, the right to receive the land goes to her heir, but the duty to pay the purchase price is imposed upon the person who receives the testator's personal property in the will.

d. **Effect of Casualty Insurance**

(1) **Common law:** At common law, where the seller had casualty insurance that covered any material physical damage during the executory period, even where the seller collected insurance proceeds, the buyer still had to pay the full purchase price.

Example: Sara agrees to sell Purpleacre to Steven for $100,000 on May 1. The closing is set for July 1. On June 1, the main structure on Purpleacre burns down. Sara collects $75,000 from the insurance company. Under the common law, Steven will still have to pay Sara the full $100,000 purchase price.

(2) **Modern view:** Modernly, where the seller has casualty insurance that covers any material, physical damage during the executory period, most jurisdictions require the seller to deduct the amount of insurance proceeds from the amount the buyer is obligated to pay.

Example: Sara agrees to sell Purpleacre to Steven for $100,000 on May 1. The closing is set for July 1. On June 1, the main structure on Purpleacre burns down. Sara collects $75,000 from the insurance company. Under the modern view, Steven will only have to pay Sara $25,000.

7. **Marketable Title**

In the absence of an agreement to the contrary, there is an implied undertaking in the contract that the vendor has a marketable title. The contract usually provides that on failure of vendor to deliver "good" and "marketable" title, the vendee may rescind and be entitled to her money.

a. **Deed Supersedes Contract:** If a deed is delivered and it contains no warranty of title, the vendee has no redress, because the deed supersedes the contract, which is no longer in effect.

b. **"Closing" Date:** The vendor is only obligated to tender a "good and marketable" title on the date when the conveyance is to be executed (i.e., "closing" date), and a *purchaser may not rescind a land sale contract before the time for performance*.

(1) **Vendor's lack of title:** Knowledge by the purchaser of the vendor's lack of title at the time she entered into the conveyance is immaterial, because she has a

right to rely upon the vendor either having a title or procuring it so as to carry out her agreement.

(2) **Remedy for unmarketable title:** Where a buyer learns that a seller's title is unmarketable before the closing, he is required to notify the seller of the defect and allow the seller a reasonable time to cure the defect. This is true even where granting of a reasonable time will extend pass the date already set for closing. The buyer is required to describe the defect in detail. Then, if the seller fails to cure, the buyer is entitled to back out of the sale. The buyer can also sue for damages for breach of land sale contract or even get specific performance with a reduction in the purchase price to reflect the defect in title.

c. **Defects Rendering Title Unmarketable:** Common defects that may render a land title unmarketable include:

(1) Outstanding mortgages or liens;

(2) The existence of restrictive covenants;

(3) Outstanding future interests of others in the property;

(4) An encumbrance which the vendor cannot or will not remove and which the vendee cannot remove by application of the purchase money;

(5) An easement upon any appreciable part of the property;

(6) Variations in the names of grantors and grantees in the chain of title;

(7) Variations in the land description in the chain of title;

(8) Outstanding dower interests;

(9) Land subject to claims of adverse possessors;

(10) Encroachments; and

(11) Existing violations of equitable servitudes or covenants.

d. **Defects that Do Not Render Title Unmarketable:** The following defects do not render title unmarketable:

(1) Zoning restrictions and

(2) Land use restrictions.

C. BOUNDARY LINE AGREEMENTS

1. **In General**

Judicial recognition is usually extended to boundary line agreements even if the agreement does not comply with the Statute of Frauds. Judicial recognition usually requires:

a. proof that the parties were not aware of the true boundary line location;

b. that there was an express or implied agreement as to its location; and

c. that possession conformed to the agreement.

Question:

Mays owns Whiteacre, a 10-acre tract used for agricultural purposes, in fee simple. On Whiteacre, Mays maintains a dwelling house for himself and his family. Mantle is the fee simple owner of Blackacre, a five-acre tract, which abuts White-acre. In 1964, Mays began to erect a concrete wall along the boundary line appurtenant to Blackacre. After Mays started to build the wall, Mantle informed him that he believed the wall was protruding onto his property. Mays informed Mantle that he paid $500.00 to have the boundary line surveyed. Mays said that the surveyor indicated that the wall did not encroach on Blackacre. Mantle accepted Mays assurances and in 1980, devised Blackacre to Snider.

After Snider entered into possession of Blackacre, he had the boundary line surveyed. The survey conclusively showed that the concrete wall extended two feet onto Blackacre. Although the encroachment does not interfere with Snider's use of Blackacre, he nevertheless demanded that Mays remove the wall. Upon Mays refusal, Snider brought an appropriate action to have the wall removed.

The most likely result is that

(A) Mays must remove the wall at his own expense
(B) Mays must remove the wall but at Snider's expense
(C) Mays may leave the wall without being liable to Snider for money damages
(D) Mays may leave the wall but he will be liable to Snider for money damages

Answer:

(C) The most common answer to this question is (D), which is incorrect. In the present case, an oral agreement made between adjoining landowners to settle an uncertain boundary line or one in dispute is valid and binding and does not come within the Statute of Frauds. Since Mantle gave Mays permission to erect the wall, Mays will not be liable to Snider (Mantle's successor in interest) for money damages. In this situation, Snider's only recourse is to sue Mantle for breach of covenant against encumbrances, which is a guarantee to the grantee that the property conveyed is not subject to outstanding rights or interests which would diminish the value of the land.

D. COVENANTS IN DEEDS RESPECTING TITLE

1. **Types of Covenants**

   The usual covenants for title include ***the covenant of seisin, the covenant of the right to convey, the covenant against encumbrances, the covenant of quiet enjoyment, and the covenant of warranty***. The covenant of further assurances is not in general use.

   a. ***A Covenant of Seisin*** is a covenant by the grantor that he owns the estate he purports to convey.

   b. ***A Covenant of the Right to Convey*** is a covenant by the grantor that he has the right to convey the estate he purports to convey.

   c. ***A Covenant Against Encumbrances*** is a covenant by the grantor that the estate he will convey is free of encumbrances. There is support for the rule that a breach of the covenant against encumbrances cannot be based upon the existence of an easement or profit known to the grantee or which was open, obvious, and notorious. The existence of a public way does not constitute a breach of a covenant against encumbrances.

   d. ***A Covenant of Warranty*** is a guarantee of title by the grantor. The grantor covenants that title is sound and agrees to defend the title against any paramount claims existing at the time of conveyance.

   e. ***A Covenant for Quiet Enjoyment*** is a covenant by the grantor that the grantee will not be disturbed in his possession or enjoyment of the property by a third party's lawful claim of title.

   f. ***A Covenant for Further Assurances*** is a covenant by the grantor to perform whatever acts may be reasonably necessary to perfect the grantee's title.

2. **Remote Parties and Covenants Running with the Land**

   The covenant of warranty, the covenant of quiet enjoyment, and the covenant of further assurances are continuous in nature and may be enforced by remote parties on the basis of privity of estate. The covenant of seisin, the covenant of the right to convey, and the covenant against encumbrances are not continuous and ***do not run with the land***. These three present covenants are breached at the time of conveyance if they are breached at all.

3. **Damages**

   The measure of damages for breach of a covenant of warranty or a covenant of seisin is the value of the consideration received by the grantor, plus interest.

   a. **Lien/Mortgage:** A lien or mortgage may cause a breach of a covenant against encumbrances. The covenantor may be liable for the amounts paid by the covenantee, not to exceed the amount received by the covenantor, in the case of an eviction or the removal of a lien.

b. **Profit/Easement:** If a profit or an easement causes a breach of a covenant against encumbrances, the measure of damages is the difference between the value of the land without the encumbrance and its value subject to the encumbrance.

E. ESTOPPEL BY DEED

1. In General

The modern doctrine of estoppel by deed is an outgrowth from the common law rules relating to warranty of title. The doctrine is based on the concept that a grantor and persons claiming ownership through him are bound by representations made concerning the title to be transferred. Some jurisdictions hold that after-acquired title by the grantor passes to the grantee by operation of law. Other jurisdictions apply the rules relating to true estoppel.

2. Deed Requirements

The doctrine of estoppel by deed applies when there is a representation respecting title expressed in the form of a warranty. It is not determined by the type of deed involved.

F. THE RECORDING SYSTEM

1. Introduction

Recording statutes only provide a means for giving constructive notice of ownership with respect to estates or interests disclosed in a recording instrument. Recording statutes may apply to mortgages, deeds, or assignments. They are applicable when two claimants both have a basis for claiming that the record titleholder of the property has conveyed, mortgaged, or assigned the property to them.

a. **An Unrecorded Instrument** is valid as between the parties to the agreement and those who do not qualify as bona fide purchasers for value and without notice.

b. **Recordation Will Not Cure the Defects** in a conveying instrument void for lack of delivery, forgery, or fraud.

c. **Adverse Possession:** Recording statutes do not apply with respect to title acquired by adverse possession.

2. Profits, Easements, and Equitable Servitudes

Recording statutes are not applicable to a profit or an easement acquired by prescription.

a. **Derivative Titles:** Recording statutes only apply in the case of derivative titles as distinguished from original titles. A derivative title is involved when the profit, easement, or equitable servitude is acquired by grant.

b. **The Physical Condition of the Land** can serve as constructive notice of an unrecorded servitude.

3. Recording Errors

A person who files an instrument to be recorded is under a duty to examine the record to verify that proper entries have been made.

4. Chain of Title

The recordation of an instrument only serves as constructive notice within its chain of title.

a. **Collateral Instrument:** A valid claim of constructive notice cannot be based upon a collateral instrument even if a grantor in the chain of title executed it.

b. **Recitals:** Constructive notice may exist based on recitals contained in recorded instruments in the chain of title.

c. **Ancestors Name:** A purchaser or mortgagee from an heir or devisee may rely on the fact that record title is in the ancestor's name.

5. Subsequent Bona Fide Purchasers

Pure notice and race-notice recording statutes only protect bona fide purchasers or mortgagees or persons claiming through such parties.

a. **Nominal Consideration** will not support the claim that a person is a *bona fide* purchaser. Partial payment of the consideration will protect the purchaser.

b. **Statutes Provide for Recordation of Acknowledged Instruments only.** Constructive notice does not arise from a recorded instrument not recorded with the prescribed formalities.

c. **Notice Will Not Be Implied** from possession consistent with the title as disclosed by the record.

d. **Temporary Possession** by a grantor does not constitute constructive notice of an interest claimed by the grantor.

6. Types of Recording Statutes

a. **Notice**

An unrecorded conveyance or other instrument *is invalid as against a subsequent bona fide purchaser("BFP") for value and without notice.* Under this type of statute, the subsequent bona fide purchaser prevails over the prior interest whether the subsequent BFP records or not. As far as the subsequent BFP is concerned, there is no premium on a race to the recorder's office. Priority is determined upon the status of the purchaser at the time the deed or mortgage is acquired.

b. **Race**

No conveyance or other instrument is valid as against purchasers (including lien creditors or other parties) for a valuable consideration, but from the time of recordation. Under this type of statute, ***the first to record wins***. A subsequent purchaser need not be bona fide and without notice since she will prevail if she records first. Priority is determined by who wins the race to the recording office.

c. **Race-Notice**

An unrecorded conveyance or other instrument is ***invalid as against a subsequent bona fide purchaser for value without notice and who records first***. This statute combines the essential features of both the notice and race type recording statutes. In order for a subsequent party to prevail in a race-notice jurisdiction, she must be both a bona fide purchaser for value without notice of the prior interest and record first.

Question:

A deed executed by A in 2002 conveyed Blackacre "for a consideration of one dollar, receipt of which was acknowledged, to B for life, then to the heirs of B." A life interest in Blackacre for the life of B is worth $20,000.00 on the date of the conveyance. The total worth of Blackacre is $50,000.00. B accepted but did not record the deed. The recording statute in this jurisdiction provided "unless recorded, all written instruments affecting title to land are void as to subsequent purchasers who paid value and without notice."

In 2006, A purported to convey Blackacre in fee simple absolute to his two sons, C and D, by warranty deed as a gift. C and D recorded the deed. Shortly thereafter, B ascertained that C and D were about to take possession of Blackacre. As a consequence, B promptly recorded his deed.

In a dispute between B and A's children as to the ownership of Blackacre, if B prevails, it will be because

(A) B paid valuable consideration for his deed
(B) B recorded his deed before A's children sought to oust him from the land
(C) C and D are not protected by the recording statute
(D) A's knowledge is imputed to his children

Answer:

(C) In order to be a *bona fide* purchaser protected under the recording act, one must (a) be subsequent, (b) pay value, (c) be without notice (the value must have actually been paid before notice), and (d) be in good faith. Be aware of the fact that recording statutes do not protect a subsequent claimant who has not paid more than a nominal consideration since he is not a purchaser. In the present case, C and D (A's children) are not protected by the recording statute because they are not purchasers. A conveyed the property to them as a gift.

VII. MORTGAGES

A. IN GENERAL

1. Definition

A *mortgage* is an interest in land created by a written instrument providing security for the performance of a duty or the payment of a debt. If the *mortgagor* does not pay the mortgage debt on time, the *mortgagee* (or the party to whom the debt is owned) has two choices. It can either assume title to the piece of real property or call the property to be sold and keep the proceeds toward satisfaction of the mortgage debt.

2. Parties Involved in Transaction

The *mortgagor* creates the mortgage. He is the "landowner" and debtor. The *mortgagee* is the creditor (e.g., bank) and the holder of the mortgage.

3. Types of Mortgage Theories

a. Lien Theory Jurisdiction

In the majority of states, the mortgage creates only a lien on the land regardless of the operative words of the mortgage instrument. Under lien theory, the mortgagor remains the owner of the land, and the mortgagee holds only a security interest in the land. Therefore, the mortgagor retains possession unless a foreclosure takes place, in which case the mortgagee may take over possession of the land.

b. Title Theory Jurisdiction

At common law, and still in about 20 states, the mortgage operates as a *conveyance of the legal title to the mortgagee*. Note, however, that such title is subject to defeasance on payment of the mortgage debt. However, under a title theory, the mortgagee is actually entitled to possession of the land at any time. Practically, this means that the mortgagee may take possession immediately upon default and need not wait for foreclosure.

c. Distinction Between Lien Theory and Title Theory

For practical purposes, the difference between lien theory and title theory states is not great. Insofar as the substantive rights of the parties are concerned, even in title theory states it is universally recognized that the mortgagee's title is only for purposes of security.

d. Intermediate Theory Jurisdiction: Very few states follow the intermediate theory which states that, while title is in the mortgagor until default, upon default, legal title switches to the mortgagee. Therefore, as in title theory jurisdictions, the mortgagee may take over possession of the property immediately upon default. Note that the difference between intermediate theory and title theory is mostly semantic.

4. **Conveyance of Encumbered Property**

Where a mortgage exists on property at the time that the mortgagor conveys the property to a third party, the language in the deed controls whether the third party assumes liability for the mortgage debt. At common law, the mortgagee could not object to the mortgagor's transfer of the property.

a. **"Subject to" Mortgage**

In a conveyance of land where the deed states that the buyer or grantee takes "subject to" a mortgage, the grantee is *not personally* liable (i.e., *in personam*) for the mortgage debt. However, if she does not pay the debt, the mortgage may be foreclosed and she (the grantee) will lose the land.

b. **"Assumption" of Mortgage**

In a sale of land in which the deed states that the purchaser "assumes" the mortgage, the purchaser or grantee *is personally liable* for the mortgage debt and is subject to a deficiency judgment in the event that a foreclosure sale does not satisfy the debt.

Note: Where the grantee assumes the mortgage but does not pay, she is primarily liable to the mortgagee, but the original mortgagor remains secondarily liable and may be called to pay if the mortgagee does not exceed as against the grantee. Note also that the mortgagee and grantee can contract so that the original mortgagor retains no liability.

c. **Deed Language Is Silent**

Where the deed language is silent, the grantee is considered to take "subject to" the mortgage.

d. **Due-On-Sale Clauses: Modern Law**

Modernly, "subject to" and "assume" do not have much relevance in deeds because a mortgagee will call in the loan and require its full payment when the mortgagor wishes to transfer ownership of the property without the mortgagee's consent. Such clauses have been deemed to be enforceable and operate almost universally in all states today.

e. **Assignments**

Mortgages are assignable. Both the mortgage (i.e., the security) and the note (i.e., the debt) are transferable.

Caveat: When there is a purported transfer of the note or debt to one party, and an assignment of the mortgage to another, the general rule is that the mortgage follows the note or debt. Be aware that the debt or note is the principal relationship, and the mortgage is only ancillary thereto for purposes of security.

f. **Recording**

The mortgage (as well as any assignments thereof) should be recorded. Failure to record the mortgage may make it possible for the mortgagor to convey to a bona fide purchaser ("BFP") who would take free of the mortgage under the recording act.

5. **Equity of Redemption**

The term ***equity of redemption*** refers to the interest of the mortgagor in a title jurisdiction after default. It was in this situation that the mortgagor needed the aid of equity to provide relief from the conveyance, which at law had become absolute in the mortgagee.

a. **Meaning of Term "Equity"**

In this situation, the term "equity" is commonly used to refer to the value of the mortgagor's interest over and above the amount of the debt owing to the mortgagee. For example, when the mortgagee under a deed transfers to a BFP, the mortgagor has no rights against the BFP, but he does have an action for redemption against the mortgagee for the value of the land or, at his election, the proceeds of the sale.

Rationale: The mortgagee now has the value of the land in his hands as a separate fund, and the mortgagor may redeem such fund as a substitute for the land.

6. **Foreclosure**

a. **Modern Day Application**

In most jurisdictions today, foreclosure is the method by which the security (i.e., the mortgaged property), or proceeds from the sale thereof, is applied to the satisfaction of the debt or obligation. It is also the means by which the mortgagee succeeds in ending the mortgagor's ownership interest in the real estate. Before a foreclosure may take place, the mortgagor must default on the loan.

b. **Right of Redemption**

The right of redemption allows a mortgagor in default to pay off the amount owed to the mortgagee and any interest prior to foreclosure. If the mortgagor actually pays off the debt prior to the foreclosure, he redeems the mortgage and takes the land free of the mortgage even though he had previously defaulted.

(1) **Equitable redemption:** Under equitable redemption, the mortgagor must redeem before the foreclosure sale. Once the foreclosure sale has occurred, the mortgagor's rights to redeem are terminated.

(2) **Statutory redemption:** Under a statutory redemption theory, a mortgagor may redeem even after the foreclosure sale has occurred. This period is usually six months to a year. About fifty percent of the states grant the mortgagor a right of statutory redemption.

(3) **Clogging:** A mortgage may not contain a provision that the mortgagor waives the right to redeem. This type of clause is called "clogging" and is invalid. If the mortgagor would like to, however, he may waive the right to redeem *after* the mortgage has been executed in exchange for good and valuable consideration.

Question:

Whitney owned a 500-acre ranch that was used for raising horses, cattle, and sheep. The property known as Rio Grande was located in west Texas. In 1995 Whitney sold Rio Grande to Cisco for the purchase price of $1,000,000. According to the terms of their land sale agreement, Cisco paid Whitney a down payment of $250,000 and Whitney agreed to carry a mortgage for the balance.

The parties then executed a mortgage as security for a $750,000 promissory note that was due in 2015 with a 7% interest per annum. The mortgage, which named Whitney as mortgagee, was properly recorded.

In 1999 Cisco defaulted on his mortgage payments and Whitney instituted a foreclosure action on the property. At the foreclosure sale Whitney, who was one of the bidders, bought back Rio Grande for $500,000. At the time of the foreclosure sale, Rio Grande had a fair market value of $1,500,000.

Two weeks later, Cisco won the Texas lottery and collected $17,000,000. He now seeks to pay off the $750,000 mortgage debt and re-acquire the property. However, Whitney has refused to honor any redemption.

Cisco has filed suit against Whitney seeking an order allowing him to pay off the mortgage (with accumulated interest) and set aside the foreclosure sale. If the court rules in favor of Cisco, it will likely be due to the fact that

(A) Cisco has an equitable right of redemption
(B) Cisco has a statutory right of redemption
(C) Whitney's purchase at the foreclosure sale clogged Cisco's right of redemption
(D) Whitney did not pay fair market value at the foreclosure sale

Answer:

(B) This same mortgage issue was tested on last summer's bar exam. Statutes providing for redemption from foreclosure sale universally permit mortgagors or their successors in interest to exercise the right. Redemption by the mortgagor "nullifies" the (foreclosure) sale in the sense that it ends the purchaser's title and restores title to the redemptioner. Osborne, **Mortgages**, pg. 641. *Remember that a redemption by the mortgagor is final; the effect is to "nullify" the foreclosure sale*. Choice (B) is correct because there must be a *statutory right to redemption* in order for Cisco to "nullify" the foreclosure sale. In choosing between (A) and (B), students need to be familiar with a brief history of mortgage remedies. At common law when a mortgagor failed to make his mortgage payment on the due date (referred to as "law day"), title to the property was forfeited. It was said that "if the mortgagor doth not pay, then the land

which he puts in pledge . . . is gone from him for ever, and so dead." Anonymous Case, 27 **Eng. Rep.** 621 (1740). The only remedy for the mortgagor was to go to equity court and request an equity of redemption (or the right to pay the loan off after "law day" or the payment day). Often, the courts would grant an extension, usually for six months. Once the courts got used to granting one extension, they sometimes granted several in a row. After this became a routine practice, lenders felt insecure in dealing with property and extending credit since the equity court had unlimited discretion in granting extensions. To protect themselves, lenders started asking for a decree to confirm their absolute title to the real property. This confirmatory decree was a decree of strict foreclosure. To "foreclose" means to shut out or bar. In this context, *what is being barred is the equity of redemption*. When we speak today of foreclosing a mortgage, the reference is really not to enforcing the lender's right but to barring the rights of the borrower in the property. Once strict foreclosure became established, borrowers asked for *a statutory right of redemption*. This referred to *the borrower's right to redeem or pay off the debt during a statutory period after the foreclosure decree*. According to this analysis, choice (A) is wrong because after the foreclosure sale technically there is no equitable right to redemption. Choice (D) is wrong because it is difficult for a mortgagor to upset a (foreclosure) sale. According to Burke, a mortgagor must show *"fraud or a gross irregularity in the conduct of the sale; the inadequacy of the sale price, standing alone, is not a basis for avoiding it. Inadequacy coupled with fraud, however, will upset the sale."* **Real Estate Transactions**, pg. 307. Choice (C) is incorrect because the term "clogging" is usually used to prevent the mortgagee from inserting terms in the mortgage instrument limiting or restricting the mortgagor's, not mortgagee's, right of redemption (e.g., a provision limiting redemption to the mortgagor himself, as distinct from his executor or heirs held invalid).

c. **Common Law or "Strict Foreclosure" View**

In early times, foreclosure meant literally foreclosing or barring the equity of redemption. It was a remedy afforded the mortgagee to prevent the mortgagor from redeeming his land after default. In other words, the mortgagee sought and obtained a decree to the effect that if the mortgagor did not satisfy the mortgage debt by a specified date, then he would be foreclosed (or barred) from ever redeeming, or getting his land back mortgage-free. This is the so-called "strict foreclosure" view and is still applicable in a minority of states.

d. **Other Methods of Foreclosure**

In some states, other methods of foreclosure (such as foreclosure under power of sale and foreclosure by entry) are available. **Note:** Foreclosure by sale under judicial supervision facilitates the determination of the value of the mortgaged property and thus aids in the determination of the amount of any deficiency decree that might be awarded where the proceeds realized from the sale are insufficient to satisfy the mortgage debt.

e. **Priority**

(1) **Typical order of priority:** Typically, chronology determines the order of priority that various mortgagees hold in the property. The first mortgagee to grant a mortgage to the mortgagor has highest priority, followed by the second

mortgagee, followed by the third, and so on. However, this order of priority may be modified in several instances: (1) where a senior mortgagee does not record his mortgage interest (see section on recording statutes); (2) where the senior mortgagee contracts away his priority to a junior mortgagee; (3) where a purchase money mortgage is in effect (see below); or (4) where the senior mortgagee changes some condition on the mortgage to make it more difficult for the mortgagor to pay.

(2) **Senior interests:** A prior mortgagee cannot be made a party against his will to a foreclosure action by a "junior mortgagee or encumbrancer." A junior mortgagee or encumbrancer is one who has granted a mortgage to the mortgagor when there was already some outstanding mortgage in place. Thus, the party who extended the original mortgage loan is called a "senior mortgagee" and any subsequent mortgagees are called "junior mortgagees."

(3) **Junior interests:** A junior encumbrancer can be made an involuntary party to a foreclosure action by a senior encumbrancer. In fact, junior encumbrancers must be made parties in order to have their claims eliminated. Where a senior mortgagee does join a junior mortgagee as a party, the junior mortgagee's right to foreclose is completely wiped out.

Note: In a foreclosure sale by a junior encumbrancer or mortgagee, the senior encumbrance or mortgage is unaffected by the proceedings.

(4) **Purchase money mortgages:** Where a mortgagor takes out a loan in order to buy property, this type of mortgage, called a "purchase money mortgage," *takes priority over other types of mortgages, even if those other types of mortgages were recorded earlier in time*.

Note: Purchase money mortgages are heavily tested on the MBE.

7. **Deficiency Judgments**

A deficiency judgment only comes into play when the mortgagor has defaulted in the mortgage debt and the mortgagee has sold the real property at a foreclosure sale. If, at the foreclosure sale, the mortgagee receives enough money for the property to pay off the mortgage debt, the mortgagor has no further obligation. However, where the proceeds from the foreclosure sale do not completely cover the mortgage debt, a deficiency is said to exist. In most states, a mortgagee may proceed directly against the mortgagor for the balance of the loan. This money needed to satisfy the mortgage loan is called a deficiency judgment.

a. **Limitations:** Many states have limitations on the amount a mortgagee may recover for a deficiency judgment. For example, some states limit the amount to the difference between the amount owed and the fair market value of the real estate when the fair market value exceeds the amount brought at the foreclosure sale. Some states even completely forbid deficiency judgment on purchase money mortgages.

8. **Installment Land Sale Contracts**

An installment land sale contract is another kind of security interest. While it is similar to a mortgage, the major difference between an installment land sale contract and a mortgage is that title to the property does not transfer to the buyer until a series of payments has been made. In other words, in a traditional mortgage, a seller sells a piece of property to a buyer, who obtains a mortgage. The buyer makes payments on a monthly basis to a mortgagee. In an installment land sale contract, the buyer makes periodic payments to the seller and does not become the owner of the property until the installments have all been paid. Therefore, the person acquiring the property makes monthly payments just as in a mortgage, but does not have an ownership interest until the debt is fully paid.

Note: Installment land sale contracts have been heavily tested recently on the MBE.

a. **Default:** In an installment land sale contract, where the buyer defaults, several different remedies apply.

   (1) **Forfeiture:** Installment land sale contracts usually require that, where a buyer does not make the required payments, she shall forfeit the property. This remedy is the most severe of the various available remedies.

   (2) **Grace period:** In many states, a buyer who defaults under an installment land sale contract is granted a grace period to pay off the loan. Such a buyer may keep the land while she is paying under a new payment schedule.

   (3) **Forfeiture and restitution:** In some states that require forfeiture of the land, the seller under the installment land sale contract is required to refund to the buyer all installments already paid, as long as these payments are more than the damages suffered by the seller.

   (4) **Foreclosure:** In some states, installment land sale contracts are treated as mortgages when the buyer is in default. In these states, the seller must actually foreclose on the property and sell the property at a foreclosure sale in order to recover money owed.

   (5) **Waiver of strict performance:** In many cases of default under an installment land sale contract, a buyer will have made late payments in the past. Where a seller has accepted those late payments, she may be deemed to have waived her right to demand timely payment. In this case, where she wishes the buyer to begin paying in a timely manner, she must send the buyer written notice and allow the buyer a reasonable amount of time to pay back payments owed.

1. Covenant Running with the Land

2. Easement

3. Defeasible Fee

4. Restraint on Alienation

5. Adverse Possession — Good and Marketable Title

6. Concurrent Ownership — Life Estate for Joint Lives

7. Adverse Possession — Tolling of the Statute

8. Joint Tenancy — Conveyance

9. Tenancy by the Entirety — Conveyance

10. Lateral/Subjacent Support of Land

11. Surface Waters — "Common Enemy Rule"

12. Trespass Above Land

13. Mortgages

14. Mortgages/Rt of Redemption

15. Easement by Implication

16. Rule in Shelley's Case

17. Rule in Shelley's Case — Abolished

18. Doctrine of Worthier Title

19. Adequacy of Land Description in Conveyance

20. Leasehold Estate — Liability of Landlord/Tenant

21. Shifting Executory Interest

22. Executory Interest *Pur Autre Vie*

23. Equitable Conversion Doctrine

24. Equitable Conversion Doctrine

25. Recording Statute/"Pure Notice"

26. Doctrine of Estoppel by Deed

27. Subsequent *Bona Fide* Purchaser — Requirements

28. Tenants in Common/Adverse Possession

29. Covenant to Pay Rent

30. Covenant to Repair

31. Covenant to Pay Fire Insurance

32. Covenant to Repair

33. Assignment — Tenant/Assignor Liability

34. Non-Assignment Clause — Landlord Waiver

35. Rent Payment — Tenant Liability

36. Tenancy for Years — Ordinary Repairs

37. Sublease — Privity of Estate

38. Eminent Domain

39. Adverse Possession — Elements of Dominion and Control

40. Covenant to Pay Taxes

41. Rent Payment — Privity of Contract

42. Sublease — Privity of Estate

43. Condemnation — Leasehold Estate

44. Non-Assignment Provision

45. Sublease — Privity

46. Privity — Landlord-Tenant
    Landlord-Subtenant

47. Landlord — Duty to Repair

48. Fee Simple Subject to Condition Subsequent

49. Profit-A-Prendre

50. Ejectment — Right of Re-entry

51. Adverse Possession

52. Adverse Possession — Tacking

53. Adverse Possession — Remainderman

54. Partition Proceedings

Questions 1–2 are based on the following fact situation.

In 2001 Wilkes was the true and record owner of Blackacre, a 150-acre tract of undeveloped land in densely populated Lovette County. Blackacre is mostly wooded except for five acres of pasture in the northeast corner that Wilkes sometimes used for cattle-grazing in connection with his dairying operation on Greenacre, an adjoining tract of land. In that year officers of the Lovette Preservation League, a newly created, non-profit corporation devoted to conservation activities, sought to negotiate with Wilkes for the purchase of Blackacre. Wilkes declined to sell because, as he said, "that land has been owned by the Wilkes family for six generations and I couldn't let it out of the family now." Further discussions, however, led to Wilkes' executing and delivering to the League (in exchange for $100,000) the following instrument:

"It is hereby agreed between the owner and the Lovette Preservation League (hereinafter "League") that from and after the date hereof (a) no entry shall be made, and no activity conducted, on Blackacre except as expressly permitted by such regulations as the League may from time to time adopt in the interest of maximum enjoyment by the public of Blackacre's virgin, natural values consistent with due protection for those values; (b) agents and employees of the League shall at all times be allowed access to Blackacre as required for the purpose of appraising the current conditions and needs of the land, and of discovering violations of the League's regulations; and (c) whenever so requested by the League, the owner shall initiate such actions at law and suits in equity, and shall file such complaints in criminal trespass and other like proceedings, as the League may reasonably require to enforce its regulations."

Wilkes continued his occasional pasturing of cattle on Blackacre until he died in 2002, leaving a will probated in that year that devised Greenacre to his friend, Rambis. The will made no mention of Blackacre, and contained no residuary clause. Wilkes' closest surviving relative was (and is) his son, Jammal. In 2003, the Lovette Preservation League wound up its affairs and transferred all its assets and property holding to the Forum Audubon Club of Greater Lovette, Inc., another non-profit conservationist organization.

1. In an appropriate action to construe the agreement between Wilkes and Lovette Preservation League, the court will determine provision (a) to be a (an)

   (A) easement
   (B) profit
   (C) covenant running with the land
   (D) negative covenant

2. In an appropriate action to construe the agreement between Wilkes and the Lovette Preservation League, the court will determine provision (b) to be a (an)

   (A) easement
   (B) profit
   (C) covenant running with the land
   (D) equitable servitude

Questions 3–4 are based on the following fact situation.

Duffy, a wealthy and devoted naturalist, owned a large and uninhabited island just a short distance off shore in Balboa Lake in the state of Dakota. Duffy permitted no pesticides or hunting on the island, and over the course of his life had bought several quite rare species of animals native to Dakota and turned them loose on the island. Among these was a magnificent albino ocelot.

Duffy lived in a large Tudor-style mansion that his grandfather, Dudley Duffy, built in 1902. Since the time the mansion was built, it has passed from father to son. In 1993, Duffy informed his attorney that he wishes to transfer ownership of the island to his daughter, Dawn. During the consultations with his attorney, Duffy indicated that he wanted the following restrictions incorporated in the instrument of conveyance: (1) all use of the island's land must be restricted to residential, non-commercial purposes; (2) no hunting of animal life on the island shall be permitted and reasonable efforts should be made to preserve the albino ocelot species; (3) the Tudor-style mansion should be repaired as needed but must never be torn down or demolished; and (4) the mansion shall never be any color except pink, the color it has been since it was built at the turn of the century.

Furthermore, Duffy told his attorney that he wanted to prevent Dawn from selling, mortgaging, or otherwise encumbering the land within Dawn's lifetime. Lastly, Duffy remarked to his attorney, "I want to keep things as simple and plain as possible; but I flat out don't want you setting up any type of trust arrangement."

3. Which of the following legal devices is most likely to be appropriate for carrying out Duffy's wishes?

   (A) equitable servitude
   (B) defeasible fee
   (C) covenant
   (D) tenancy at will

4. Regardless of which legal device is used in the preceding question, which of Duffy's objectives is LEAST likely to be upheld?

   (A) restriction to use of the island for residential purposes
   (B) restriction prohibiting the hunting of animals on the island
   (C) restriction requiring the mansion to be painted only the color of pink
   (D) restriction on the sale, mortgage, or other encumbrance on the land

Question 5 is based on the following fact situation.

For many months, Drew had been negotiating with Rollins for the purchase of Treeacre. Finally, on August 18, 2001 Drew and Rollins entered into a real estate sales contract which provided in part: "I, Rollins, agree to convey good and marketable title to Drew sixty days from the date of this contract." The stated purchase price for Treeacre was $175,000.

On October 11, 2001, Drew telephoned Rollins and told him that his title search indicated that Wilkins, not Rollins, was the owner of record to the property. Rollins responded that, notwithstanding the state of the record, he had been in adverse possession for twenty-one years. The statutory period of adverse possession in this jurisdiction is twenty years.

The next day Drew conducted an investigation which revealed that Rollins had in fact been in adverse possession of Treeacre for twenty-one years. At the time set for closing, Rollins tendered a deed in the form agreed in the sales contract. Drew, however, refused to pay the purchase price or take possession of Treeacre because of Rollins' inability to convey "good and marketable title."

5. In an appropriate action by Rollins against Drew for specific performance, the vendor will

   (A) prevail, because he has obtained "good and marketable title" by adverse possession
   (B) prevail, because Rollins' action for specific performance is an action *in rem* to which Wilkins is not a necessary party
   (C) not prevail, because an adverse possessor takes title subject to an equitable lien from the dispossessed owner
   (D) not prevail, because Drew cannot be required to buy a lawsuit even if the probability is great that Drew would prevail against Rollins

Question 6 is based on the following fact situation.

Testator owns Pineview in fee simple. Testator executes and delivers a deed to Pineview with the following granting clause:

"To Peter and Paula for their joint lives and upon the death of the first of them to die to the survivor, but if Patrick outlives both of them, then to Patrick."

6. As a result of the grant, which of the following is the most accurate statement regarding the ownership rights of Pineview?

(A) Peter and Paula are joint tenants in fee simple defeasible, and Patrick has an executory interest.
(B) Peter and Paula have a joint life estate for the life of the one who lives the longest, and Peter, Paula, and Patrick have contingent remainders.
(C) Peter and Paula are tenants in common for the life of the first of them to die, Peter and Paula have contingent remainders in fee simple defeasible, and Patrick has an executory interest.
(D) There is no legal difference between the results reached in alternatives (A), (B), or (C).

Question 7 is based on the following fact situation.

Luzinski was the fee simple owner of Grassacre, a 20-acre tract located in northern Iowa. When Luzinski moved to Florida, Fisk took possession of Grassacre. Fisk's possession has at all times complied with the requirements of the applicable adverse possession statute in effect.

Twelve years after Fisk took possession, Luzinski died intestate, leaving Carlton, his six-year-old son, as his only surviving heir. Nine years after Luzinski's death when Carlton was fifteen, Law, who was Carlton's guardian, discovered that Fisk was in possession of Grassacre. In Iowa the statutory period of adverse possession is twenty years and the age of majority is eighteen.

7. Which of the following correctly describes the state of title to Grassacre?

(A) Fisk has acquired title by adverse possession.
(B) Fisk will not acquire title unless he continues in adverse possession for an additional three years, or until Carlton reaches the age of eighteen.
(C) Fisk will not acquire title unless he continues in adverse possession for an additional eight years, making a total of twelve years after Luzinski's death.
(D) Fisk will not acquire title unless he continues in adverse possession for an additional twelve years, or nine years after Carlton attains the age of eighteen.

Questions 8–9 are based on the following fact situation.

Wanda and Hugo own Blackacre as joint tenants.

8. If Wanda transfers her interest by quitclaim deed to Louis, without Hugo's knowledge, what interest, if any, does Louis have in Blackacre?

(A) no interest
(B) an undivided one-half interest with right of survivorship
(C) an undivided one-half interest without right of survivorship
(D) a lien against the entire property

9. Assume for the purposes of this question only that Wanda and Hugo are married and own Blackacre as tenants by the entirety. If Wanda transfers her interest in Blackacre by quitclaim deed to Louis, without Hugo's knowledge, what interest, if any, does Louis have?

   (A) no interest
   (B) an undivided one-half interest with right of survivorship
   (C) an undivided one-half interest without right of survivorship
   (D) a lien against the entire property

Questions 10–12 are based on the following fact situation.

X, Y, and Z are the owners of three contiguous lots in the City of Palm Grove. A downward slope exists from X's land to Z's land.

X's and Y's lots were in an unimproved natural state. Z, however, had lived for ten years in a house which he had built on his property.

In 1990, X planted trees and shrubbery on his land along the boundary of Y's lot.

In 1991, Y, in preparation for building a house on his lot, carefully made an excavation eight feet deep for the purpose of building a basement. The west side of the excavation, which was five feet east of the X-Y boundary, suddenly collapsed and a quantity of X's soil, trees, and shrubbery fell into the hole. Y hauled away the debris.

Y completed construction of his house and macadamized an area for use as a driveway, without changing the former contours of the land. Shortly thereafter, Z began to make complaints to Y about the flooding of his basement, which he claimed had been previously free of water.

10. In an appropriate action by X against Y to recover for the damage to his land, judgment for whom?

    (A) Y, if he was conducting the excavation work non-negligently
    (B) Y, because he was under no duty to support X's land in its improved state
    (C) X, because a landowner is entitled to support of his land in its natural condition
    (D) X, because a landowner has an absolute right to have his land supported by the neighboring land

11. Assume for the purposes of this question only that Z builds a concrete wall three feet along his border with Y to prevent the flow of rain water running onto his land from Y's property. This causes the surface water to stand and become stagnant on the northerly corner of Y's land. Y demanded that Z remove the wall and upon Z's refusal, Y brought an appropriate action to compel removal. The most likely result is

    (A) Z must remove the wall because he has no right to obstruct the flow of such surface water
    (B) Z must remove the wall at Y's expense
    (C) Z may leave the wall without being liable to Y for money damages
    (D) Z may leave the wall but he will be liable to Y for money damages

12. Assume for the purposes of this question only that Y became engaged in experimentation with artificial means to seed clouds in an attempt to suppress damaging rain storms. The rain storms apparently originated in and over the area within which Z's land is located. Z brought suit to enjoin such cloud seeding activity. At trial, it was found that Y had been conducting its activities over clouds above Z's land. According to further testimony, Y's seeding operations did, in fact, cause the complete dissipation of the clouds. The court should

(A) enjoin Y's seeding operations because it constitutes an unreasonable interference with the space above Z's land
(B) enjoin Y's seeding operations because one does not have the right to interfere with natural rainfall
(C) not enjoin Y's seeding operations if they were necessary to protect his property from the rain storms
(D) not enjoin Y's seeding operations because Z does not own the space above his land

Questions 13–14 are based on the following fact situation.

Quirk owned a four-story office building located in downtown El Paso. The building, named Quirk Towers, was old and badly in need of renovation. To finance the improvements, Quirk borrowed $125,000 from his friend, Lama. As consideration for the loan, Quirk executed a promissory note for $125,000 payable to Lama in one year and secured by a mortgage on Quirk Towers. The mortgage was dated January 1, 1999, and was recorded January 2, 1999. Thereafter, on February 1, 1999, Quirk executed a deed absolute on Quirk Towers and named Lama as grantee. This deed, although absolute in form, was intended only as additional security for the payment of the debt. In order to make judicial foreclosure unnecessary and to eliminate the right to redeem, Quirk then delivered the deed to Uribe in escrow with instructions to deliver the deed to Lama if Quirk failed to pay his promissory note at maturity.

On January 1, 2000, Quirk failed to pay the note when it came due. Thereupon, Uribe, in accordance with escrow instructions, delivered Quirk's deed on the office building to Lama, which he promptly and properly recorded. Two weeks later, Quirk tendered the $125,000 indebtedness to Lama. When Lama refused to accept it, Quirk brought an appropriate action to set aside and cancel the deed absolute and to permit the redemption of Quirk Towers from Lama. Conversely, Lama counterclaimed to quiet title and argued that the deed absolute was intended as an outright conveyance upon default.

13. The court should enter a judgment that will grant the relief sought by

(A) Quirk, but only if Quirk can establish that the mortgage takes precedence over the deed absolute since it was executed earlier in time
(B) Quirk, because the deed absolute did not extinguish his right of redemption
(C) Lama, because the deed absolute effectuated an outright conveyance that extinguished the redemption interest sought to be retained by Quirk
(D) Lama, because Quirk is estopped to deny the effect of the deed absolute in conjunction with the escrow arrangement

14. For this question only, assume the following facts. On January 1, 2000, Quirk failed to pay the note when it came due. The next day, Uribe, the escrow agent, delivered the deed to Quirk Towers to Lama. Lama then properly recorded this deed on January 3. One week later, on January 10, Lama conveyed Quirk Towers by warranty deed to Gonzales for the purchase price of $200,000. On January 12, Quirk tendered the $125,000 balance due to Lama, which he refused to accept. Quirk now brings an appropriate action against Lama and Gonzales to set aside the conveyance and to permit the redemption of the property by Quirk. Which of the following best states Quirk's legal rights, if any, in his action against Lama and Gonzales?

(A) Quirk has no rights against Gonzales but Quirk does have an action for redemption against Lama for the value of the property.

(B) Quirk has no rights against Lama but Quirk does have an action for redemption against Gonzales for the value of the property.

(C) Quirk has the option of seeking redemption against either Lama or Gonzales for the value of the property but Quirk cannot set aside the conveyance.

(D) Quirk has no rights against either Lama or Gonzales because he defaulted on the promissory note.

Question 15 is based on the following fact situation.

Fegen owned two adjacent ten-story commercial buildings in Beverly Hills. The buildings were respectively known as Trump Towers and Galleria Plaza. The first floors of both buildings were occupied by various retail establishments. The buildings' other floors were rented to tenants and used as offices. There was an enclosed walkway which connected the second floor of each building. Thus, shoppers and office workers could walk across the common walkway and gain access to each building.

While the buildings were being used in this manner, Fegen sold Trump Towers to Toyota by warranty deed, which made no mention of any rights concerning the walkway. The walkway continued to be used by the occupants of both buildings. Thereafter, the walkway became unsafe as a consequence of wear and tear.

As a result, Toyota hired a contractor to repair the walkway area. When Fegen saw the contractor removing the carpeting along the walkway, he demanded that Toyota discontinue the repair work. After Toyota refused, Fegen brought an action to enjoin Toyota from continuing the work.

15. The most likely result will be a decision for

(A) Fegen, because Toyota does not have rights in the walkway

(B) Fegen, because Toyota's rights in Trump Towers do not extend to the walkway

(C) Toyota, because Toyota has an easement in the walkway, and an implied right to keep the walkway in repair

(D) Toyota, because he has a right to take whatever action is necessary to protect himself from possible tort liability from persons using the walkway

Questions 16–18 are based on the following fact situation.

In 1956, Obie conveyed Blackacre to John "for life, remainder after John's death to his heirs." Two years later John entered into a real estate agreement for the sale of Blackacre to Ed, whereby John agreed to convey the premises to Ed in fee simple absolute. Prior to the settlement date, Ed contacted John, telling him that he would not perform his part of the agreement because John could not convey a fee simple.

16. If the Rule in Shelley's Case is followed in this jurisdiction, the outcome of a suit by John for specific performance of the real estate contract would result in

    (A) John not succeeding, since he could not convey marketable title
    (B) John succeeding, because he had a fee simple to convey
    (C) John not succeeding, because his heirs have to join in the transaction in order to convey marketable title
    (D) John succeeding, because the conveyance of his life estate divested the contingent remainder of his heirs

17. Assume for the purposes of this question only that Shelley's Rule has been abolished by statute in this jurisdiction. Thus, John's prayer for specific performance would now be

    (A) denied, since the Rule would not be triggered, thus creating only a life estate in John
    (B) granted, since the remainder in his heirs would become vested into a full fee in those heirs
    (C) granted, since John's heirs receive a vested indefeasible interest in Blackacre
    (D) denied, since under the Doctrine of Worthier Title, at the termination of John's life estate, the grantor has a reversionary interest

18. Assume for the purposes of this question only that Obie conveyed Blackacre to John "for life, with remainder to Obie's heirs." Later John conveyed Blackacre to Sam "for as long as he would continue to farm the property." After John's death, Obie's heirs brought suit against Sam to quiet title. Which Common Law doctrine would be most applicable in the court's determination of the ownership of Blackacre?

    (A) Rule of Wild's Case
    (B) Doctrine of Destructibility of Contingent Remainders
    (C) Doctrine of Worthier Title
    (D) Rule against Remainders in the Grantees' Heirs

Question 19 is based on the following fact situation.

Rockne Faust owned Scenicacre, a 40-acre tract of farmland which was located in the township of South Bend. Rockne leased the property and building thereon to Dan Devine for a term of seven years commencing on February 15, 1990 and terminating at 12 noon on February 15, 1997. The lease contained the following provision: "Lessee covenants to pay the rent of $1,000 per month on the fifteenth day of each month and to keep the building situated upon said leased premises in as good repair as it was at the time of said lease until the expiration thereof." The lease also contained a provision giving Devine the option to purchase 10 acres of Scenicacre for $30,000 at the expiration of the lease term. Before the lease was executed, Faust orally promised Devine that he (Faust) would have the 10-acre tract surveyed.

During the last year of the lease Devine decided to exercise the option to purchase the 10 acres of Scenicacre. Without Faust's knowledge, Devine began to build an irrigation ditch across the northern section of the property. When Devine notified Faust that he planned to exercise the option, Faust refused to perform. Faust also informed Devine that he never had the 10-acre tract surveyed.

19. If Devine brings suit for specific performance, which of the following is Faust's best defense?

    (A) The option agreement was unenforceable under the parole evidence rule.
    (B) Faust's failure to survey the 10-acre tract excused him from further obligations under the contract.
    (C) The description of the property was too indefinite to permit the remedy sought.
    (D) The option was unenforceable because it lacked separate consideration.

Question 20 is based on the following fact situation.

Lord was the owner of a large high-rise apartment building in Detroit. On June 1, 2001, Mr. and Mrs. Tenner took possession of a three-bedroom apartment in Lord's building under a three-year lease to them from Lord at a rental of $825 per month. Their lease (as all other leases given by Lord) contained the following provisions:

> "Tenants hereby agree that ... the premises are not to be occupied by any two or more persons not related to one another by blood or marriage ..."

> "The term of this lease shall be three years from the date hereof as long as all the agreements herein shall be faithfully performed."

Mr. and Mrs. Tenner lived in the apartment for two years. On June 10, 2003, however, a fire destroyed the apartment building. As a result, all the apartments in the building were rendered uninhabitable. After Mr. and Mrs. Tenner were dispossessed from their apartment, Lord brought suit against them to recover the rent due for the balance of the lease. Mr. and Mrs. Tenner claim that they are no longer liable for rent or any other obligations under the lease. The Lord-Tenner leasehold contract contained no provision regarding liability for fire.

20. If the decision is in favor of Mr. and Mrs. Tenner, it will be because

    (A) there was nothing in the lease regarding liability for fire
    (B) Mr. and Mrs. Tenner did not own an interest in the property
    (C) Lord should not be unjustly enriched
    (D) Lord did not contract to convey the property to Mr. and Mrs. Tenner

Questions 21–22 are based on the following fact situation.

In 2002, John Jones executed a deed by which he conveyed Blackacre for a consideration of one dollar, receipt of which was acknowledged, "to Burkhart for life, then to Carr for life but if Carr moves to another state, to Drew for the life of Carr, then to the heirs of Carr if Carr does not move to another state and to the heirs of Drew if Carr does move to another state." This deed was promptly recorded.

21. During Burkhart's lifetime, Carr's interest may best be described as a (an)

    (A) contingent remainder
    (B) shifting executory interest
    (C) vested remainder subject to complete divestiture
    (D) vested remainder subject to partial divestiture

22. During Burkhart's lifetime, Drew's interest may best be described as a (an)

    (A) estate *pur autre vie*
    (B) contingent remainder *pur autre vie*
    (C) vested remainder *pur autre vie*
    (D) shifting executory interest *pur autre vie*

Question 23 is based on the following fact situation.

In 1970, Rufus Reefer owned Grassacre, a thirty-acre tract located just inside Weedville in Humboldt County. Grassacre included the family home, The Rookery, a decaying antebellum mansion complete with tennis courts, stables, and a smaller second house which once was occupied by tenants who farmed Grassacre. The second house, however, had long been vacant as a result of the economic decay of Humboldt County.

Prosperity burst upon Weedville in 1971, and Reefer began selling acre lots in Grassacre. By 1978, Reefer had sold twenty five acres, retaining five acres which included The Rookery, tennis courts, stables, and the former tenants' house.

On May, 19, 1979, Reefer entered into a valid written contract with Doper. According to the terms of their agreement, Reefer agreed to sell and convey his remaining interest in Grassacre for a consideration of $500,000. The land sale contract provided a closing date of November 19, 1979 and stipulated that "time was of the essence."

On July 2, 1979, a fire destroyed The Rookery. Reefer had The Rookery insured for $450,000 against fire loss and collected that amount from the insurance company. At the closing on November 19th, Doper tendered a cashier's check for $50,000 and demanded a deed conveying a fee simple interest in the property. Conversely, Reefer tendered a deed of conveyance and demanded the full purchase price of $500,000. Doper refused Reefer's demand.

23. In an appropriate action for specific performance against Doper, Reefer demanded $500,000. If Reefer prevails, which of the following is the best rationale for the outcome?

(A) The fact that The Rookery was insured for $450,000 is irrelevant.
(B) Reefer and Doper each had an insurable interest in the property.
(C) The doctrine of equitable conversion has been abolished.
(D) The doctrine of equitable conversion requires such a result.

Question 24 is based on the following fact situation.

On November 1, 2001, Beeson contracted to purchase from Sloan for $250,000 certain property on which was erected a hotel. The contract required Beeson to pay Sloan a deposit of $12,500 with the balance of the purchase price payable at closing on December 1, 2001. On November 24, 2001, a fire caused the hotel to burn down.

As a consequence, Beeson refused to honor the contract. Sloan now brings an action for specific performance arguing that the doctrine of equitable conversion places the loss on the buyer. Beeson argues that to enforce the contract would be harsh and oppressive to him.

24. If judgment is for Beeson, it will be because

(A) Sloan assumed the risk
(B) Sloan would be unjustly enriched
(C) legal title remained in Sloan
(D) equity will relieve Beeson of a bad bargain

Question 25 is based on the following fact situation.

The state of Runnymede has the following recording statute in effect:

> "No conveyance is good against a subsequent purchaser for a valuable consideration and without notice, unless the same be recorded prior to subsequent purchase."

Lau is the owner in fee simple of Blackacre, a 20-acre tract of unimproved land situated in Madison, Runnymede. On May 1, Lau sold Blackacre to Eto for the purchase price of $40,000 under a quitclaim deed. Eto did not record the deed. On May 5, Lau died leaving a valid will by which he devised Blackacre to his son, Landon. After the administration of Lau's estate, Landon, in consideration of the sum of $75,000, conveyed Blackacre to Fong by warranty deed. This transaction took place on August 1. When Fong acquired title to Blackacre, he had no actual knowledge of Eto's deed (which was still unrecorded). On August 10, Eto recorded his deed to Blackacre. Fong did not record the deed he received from Landon until August 15.

25. In an appropriate action to quiet title to Blackacre, in which all interested parties have been joined, title will be found to be in

    (A) Eto, because his deed preceded Fong's deed
    (B) Eto, because his deed was recorded prior to Fong's deed
    (C) Fong, because he is protected by the recording statute
    (D) Fong, because he took title by warranty deed and Eto took title by quitclaim deed

Question 26 is based on the following fact situation.

A deed executed by A in 1997 conveyed Blackacre for a consideration of one dollar, receipt of which was acknowledged, "to B for life, then to the heirs of B." A life interest in Blackacre for the life of B is worth $20,000 on the date of the conveyance. The total worth of Blackacre is $50,000. B accepted but didn't record the deed. The recording statute in this jurisdiction provided "unless recorded all written instruments affecting title to land are void as to subsequent purchasers who paid value and without notice."

In 2001 A purported to convey Blackacre in fee simple absolute to his two sons, C and D, by a warranty deed as a gift. C and D recorded the deed. Shortly thereafter, B ascertained that C and D were about to take possession of Blackacre. As a consequence, B promptly recorded his deed.

26. In a dispute between B and A's children as to the ownership of Blackacre, if B prevails it will be because

    (A) B paid valuable consideration for his deed
    (B) B recorded his deed before A's children sought to oust him from the land
    (C) C and D are not protected by the recording statute
    (D) A's knowledge is imputed to his children

Question 27 is based on the following fact situation.

Fletcher, a noted conservationist, died four years ago leaving a will by which he devised Greenacre, a 100-acre tract, to his daughter, Fawn. At the time of Fletcher's death, he believed that he owned all of Greenacre. However, Fletcher actually owned ninety-five acres of Greenacre. The other five acres were owned by Oswald. After taking possession of Greenacre, Fawn executed and delivered a warranty deed to Scott purporting to convey all 100 acres of Greenacre. The agreed purchase price was $100,000. According to the terms of the sale, Scott paid Fawn a down payment of $25,000 with the unpaid portion of the purchase price (i.e. $75,000) secured by a mortgage. The mortgage instrument described the property interest as covering all 100 acres of Greenacre.

After the Fawn-Scott transaction was completed, Oswald came forward and informed the parties that she was the true record owner of five acres of Greenacre. Upon Oswald's threat to sue to quiet title, Fawn negotiated a deal whereby she paid Oswald $5,000 for the five-acre tract. As part of their agreement, Oswald executed and delivered a quitclaim deed quitclaiming to Scott all of her interest in the five-acre parcel.

Thereafter, Scott defaulted on the mortgage debt and Fawn properly consummated foreclosure proceedings, becoming the purchaser of Greenacre at her own foreclosure sale. The description of the deed in the foreclosure sale referred to Greenacre as consisting of all 100-acres. After the foreclosure sale was finalized, Scott brought suit claiming title in fee simple to the five-acre tract, formerly owned by Oswald.

27. In an appropriate action to determine the title to the said five-acre tract, Scott will

(A) lose, because Fawn did not have good and marketable title at the time she purported to convey Greenacre to Scott
(B) lose, because the doctrine of after-acquired title controls
(C) win, because the deed from Oswald to Scott was a quitclaim deed
(D) win, because the quitclaim deed from Oswald to Scott was subsequent to the deed from Fawn to Scott and to the mortgage

Question 28 is based on the following fact situation.

Wilson, being fee simple owner of Blackacre, devised it to his daughter, Jennifer, and her husband, Brad, as tenants by the entirety. Jennifer and Brad took immediate possession of Blackacre and lived there with their children, Beth and Jeffrey. Thereafter, Brad died in an automobile accident. In 1952, two years after her father's death, Beth moved to another state.

Jeffrey lived with his mother on Blackacre until her death intestate in 1960. He continued in exclusive possession of Blackacre until his death in 1981. In his will, Jeffrey devised Blackacre to the Boy Scouts of America. Jeffrey was unaware that Beth was still alive and that title to Blackacre had descended to the two of them as their mother's sole surviving heirs. Since his mother's death in 1960, Jeffrey has held himself out as the owner of Blackacre, maintaining it and paying all of the taxes on the property. Beth has not communicated with either her mother or Jeffrey since her redomiciling in 1952. The jurisdiction in which Blackacre is located has a 20-year limitation period for the acquisition of property by adverse possession.

28. What interest, if any, does Beth have in the property?

    (A) none, because of her own laches
    (B) none, because Jeffrey acquired title to Blackacre by adverse possession
    (C) an undivided one-half interest because Jeffrey's possession was not adverse to Beth's title
    (D) an undivided one-half interest because the 2-year limitation period did not run against her since she was unaware of Jeffrey's exclusive possession

Questions 29–30 are based on the following fact situation.

Landlord owns a three-story building which is located in the township of Scotch Plains. Landlord leased the building and the surrounding property to Tenant for a term of six years commencing on December 1, 1995 and terminating on November 30, 2001. Their leasehold agreement contained the following provisions: "Tenant covenants to pay the rent of $500 per month on the first day of each month and to keep the building situated upon leased premises in as good repair as it was at the time of said lease until the expiration thereof."

On April 15, 1996 Neighbor, owner of an adjoining parcel of land, was burning leaves and underbrush on his land. There was a high wind blowing in the direction of the land which Landlord leased to Tenant and the wind carried the burning leaves onto Tenant's property. The building caught fire and caused $150,000 in fire damages. Tenant has not occupied the leased premises since the date of the fire because the building was rendered uninhabitable.

NOTE: Scotch Plains is a common law jurisdiction. In addition, the controlling Scotch Plains Statute of Limitations for initiating an action for damages due to negligence is five years from the time the cause of damage occurs.

29. On May 1, 1996 Landlord brings suit against Tenant asserting breach of contract. Judgment for

    (A) Landlord, since a tenant remains liable to pay rent even though as a result of the fire, the property was rendered uninhabitable
    (B) Landlord, since the covenant to pay rent runs with the land
    (C) Tenant, as it would be inequitable to enforce the rental provision in the lease because the premises was rendered uninhabitable
    (D) Tenant, since an increasing number of states have enacted statutes relieving a tenant of his obligation to pay rent where the premises are rendered uninhabitable by fire or other acts of God

30. In an appropriate action to construe Tenant's obligation under the covenant to keep the premises in repair, which of the following is the most accurate statement?

    (A) Tenant is liable for normal wear and tear under the covenant to repair.
    (B) Tenant is liable under such a covenant for all defects, including the acts of God.
    (C) Tenant's covenant to repair is void as against public policy, since the landlord is under an affirmative duty to make repairs on the demised premises.
    (D) Tenant's duty to keep the premises in good repair relieves the landlord of his obligation to disclose the existence of any latent defects.

Questions 31–34 are based on the following fact situation.

Harry is the owner in fee simple of a tract of land on which is situated a large office building. Harry leases the land and building thereon to Tony for a term of seven years, commencing on August 1, 1994, and terminating at midnight on July 31, 2001. The lease contains the following provisions:

"(1) Tony covenants not to assign the leased premises without the consent of Harry;

(2) Tony covenants to pay the rent of $750 per month on the first day of each month;

(3) Tony covenants to keep the leased premises in repair;

(4) Tony covenants to keep the building on the leased premises insured against fire in the amount of $100,000; and

(5) Harry covenants to utilize any fire insurance proceeds for repair or replacement only."

After three years of the lease had expired, Tony, without the consent of Harry, assigned the entire balance of the lease period to Rick, who took immediate possession of the leased property. Harry accepted rental payments from Rick. Then in 1998, Rick assigned his leasehold interest to Simon. Simon went into possession, but failed to pay any rent for two months. Soon afterwards, a fire spread from an adjoining building to the leased property, completely destroying the building thereon.

It was established that the owner of the premises on which the fire started had failed for several years to comply with the municipal Fire Code measures applicable to his building. While Tony was in possession of the leased property, he carried a fire insurance policy on the premises in the amount of $100,000. However, Tony allowed the policy to lapse after his assignment to Rick. Rick did carry insurance on the leased building, but only in the amount of $50,000. When Simon took possession of the building, he did not obtain any fire insurance.

31. Harry learned that the building was not insured at the time of the fire. In an action by Harry against Tony to recover for the fire loss, Harry will most probably

(A) recover, since in accordance with the Rule in Spencer's Case, the covenant to maintain fire insurance would "touch and concern" the land

(B) recover, since Tony's obligation to maintain fire insurance did not terminate after his assignment to Rick

(C) not recover, since the covenant to provide fire insurance did not run with the land

(D) not recover, since Simon, as assignee, would be liable for the fire loss

32. Which of the following is the most accurate statement regarding a tenant's covenant to keep the premises in repair?

(A) A tenant is liable for normal wear and tear under the covenant to repair.

(B) A tenant is liable under such a covenant for all defects, including the acts of God.

(C) A tenant's covenant to repair is void as against public policy, since the landlord is under an affirmative duty to make repairs on the demised premises.

(D) The tenant's duty to keep the premises in good repair relieves the landlord of his obligation to disclose the existence of any latent defects.

33. After Simon failed to make his rental payments for the first two months of his lease, Harry brought suit against Tony to recover for the unpaid rent. Judgment for

    (A) Harry, since Tony's contractual obligation under the lease survived the assignments
    (B) Harry, since he did not object to the assignments
    (C) Tony, since Simon, as assignee, would only be held liable
    (D) Tony, since his assignment to Rick constituted a novation, thereby extinguishing his obligation to pay rent

34. Assume for the purposes of this question only that Harry, after learning of Rick's assignment to Simon, brings suit against Rick to have the assignment declared void. Harry will most likely

    (A) succeed, since the original leasehold agreement prohibited assignments
    (B) succeed, since the covenant prohibiting assignments did not run with the land
    (C) not succeed, since in accordance with the Rule in Dumpor's Case, where the landlord consents to one transfer, he waives his right to avoid future transfers
    (D) not succeed, since the privity of estate between Rick and Harry terminated when he assigned the leasehold to Simon

Questions 35–37 are based on the following fact situation.

Leonard, the owner of a two-story dwelling house, leased it completely furnished to Thomas for a ten-year period. Towards the end of the seventh year of the term, a violent storm blew off several of the roof shingles. Thomas noticed a leak through the roof where the shingles had blown off, but didn't make any repairs. A month later, a severe rain storm occurred and water leaked through the roof causing damage to the valuable parquet floors in the two rooms below. Before the term of his lease ended, Thomas discovered that Leonard had not paid his taxes on the property, so he purchased the property through a sheriff's sale. Thomas refuses to make any further rental payments on the property.

35. If Leonard brings suit against Thomas for payment of rent in arrears, he would most likely

    (A) succeed, because the tenant is estopped to deny Leonard's title
    (B) succeed, because of his security interest in the property
    (C) fail, because the purchase by Thomas vitiated any further contractual obligations
    (D) fail, because he was under a duty to keep the demised premises in reasonably good repair

36. In a subsequent proceeding by Leonard against Thomas to recover for the damage to the parquet floors resulting from the leak, liability would most likely be imposed upon

    (A) Leonard, because he was under an implied obligation to keep the premises in a habitable condition
    (B) Leonard, because he was under an affirmative obligation to deliver the premises in a reasonable state of repair
    (C) Leonard, because of the contractual obligation under the lease to make all necessary repairs during the term of the lease
    (D) Thomas, because a tenant for years is obligated to make such ordinary repairs on the leased property

37. Assume for the purposes of this question only that two years after Thomas entered into the leasehold agreement with Leonard, he subleases the house to Steve. Thereafter, Steve defaults on the rental payments. If Leonard brings an action to recover the past rent due from Steve, Leonard will

    (A) recover, because privity of estate exists between a landlord and sublessee
    (B) recover, because there is privity of contract between a landlord and sublessee
    (C) recover, because there is both privity of estate and privity of contract between a landlord and sublessee
    (D) not recover, because privity of estate does not exist between the landlord and sublessee

Question 38 is based on the following fact situation.

Recreational Systems, Inc., under the authority of a statute of the State of Greenora, sued to have condemned 1000 acres of forested land owned by the Great Lakes Timber Co., which it planned to develop for use as a state recreational area and state gamelands. After a hearing, the state court ordered possession of the land surrendered to Recreational Systems, prior to determination of compensation, upon deposit in court of a sum deemed adequate to cover damages which might be awarded. Great Lakes Timber Co. immediately commenced an action to enjoin the court-ordered sale of their property.

38. Which of the following would be the best ground for upholding the state court's order?

    (A) The power of eminent domain may only be delegated directly to a private enterprise for a public related use or activity.
    (B) The power of eminent domain may only be delegated to a public authority through a legislative determination.
    (C) The injured party has not proved such irreparable injury to use as amounts to a "taking."
    (D) The Fifth Amendment power of eminent domain incorporated by the Fourteenth Amendment as applicable to the States does not require that payment be made prior to condemnation of the property.

Question 39 is based on the following fact situation.

Southhampton is a state with a long stretch of scenic, ecologically unique, and relatively unspoilt sea coast. Most of the coastline is privately owned by persons who have permanent or vacation residences on their coastal lands. In 1954 Little purchased a two-acre tract of littoral (i.e. coastal) land in Southhampton. When Little bought the property, there was a narrow concrete walkway (about 20 feet in length and five feet in width) adjoining the land. The walkway, which was designed to provide pedestrian access to the beach, was owned by the Southhampton Coastal Commission. When Little moved into his beach house in 1954, he noticed that the walkway was rarely used. As a result, Little decided to enclose the walkway and construct a paddle ball court over the entire area. He did so without notifying the state Coastal Commission. He has continued to use this area in excess of the period required for adverse possession.

39. In an appropriate action brought by Little to establish title to the walkway area, which of the following must be establish if he is to prevail?

    I. Real property interests can be abandoned by a governmental entity without an official vote.
    II. Lack of use of the walkway by the state created an irrevocable license in him.
    III. Real property interests can be lost by a state by adverse possession.
    IV. His use of the walkway area is proof of his intent to assert dominion over that section.

    (A) I and II only
    (B) I and III only
    (C) II and IV only
    (D) III and IV only

Questions 40–43 are based on the following fact situation.

Donaldson, an owner in fee simple, leased a three-story house to McQuirk for a term of ten years. By the terms of the lease McQuirk expressly covenanted to pay a monthly rental of $300 and to pay the taxes on the premises during the term of the lease. The lease also stipulated that McQuirk, as lessee, may not assign or sublease the said premises.

McQuirk and his family lived in the house for two years. Then McQuirk, still owing Donaldson three months back rent, assigned his leasehold interest in the property to Moore, who was unaware of the prohibition against assignments. This written assignment expressly provided that Moore would pay Donaldson the monthly rental of $300 but was silent concerning the payment of taxes. Donaldson never objected to this assignment. Six months after the assignment, Donaldson conveyed his property interest in the premises to Davis.

After residing in the house for a year, Moore subleased the third floor to Burger for a term of two years; the agreement provided that Moore would receive a monthly rental payment of $100.

40. Moore failed to pay the taxes on the property. Davis, after paying the taxes, brought suit against Moore for the amount paid. Judgment would be for

    (A) Davis
    (B) Moore, since he did not contract with McQuirk to pay the taxes on the property
    (C) Moore, since the covenant to pay taxes will not "run with the land" unless the intent is clearly expressed in the original lease
    (D) Moore, since the covenant to pay taxes is merely collateral and does not "run with the land"

41. After McQuirk's assignment to Moore, Donaldson sues McQuirk to recover the rent in arrears. Donaldson will most likely

    (A) succeed, because Donaldson and McQuirk stood in privity of contract
    (B) succeed, even though he had notice of the assignment
    (C) not succeed, because McQuirk had assigned his interest in the premises before Donaldson brought suit
    (D) not succeed, because he did not object to the assignment

42. After Burger had made regular rental payments to Moore for the first six months of the sub-lease, he defaulted. The following month, Moore sent Davis $200 as payment for rent and notified him that he should collect the remaining $100 from Burger, who refused to vacate the premises. In an action by Davis against Burger to recover the additional $100 for rent due, he will most probably

    (A) recover, since the landlord and sublessee are in privity of estate
    (B) recover, even though he never objected to the sublease
    (C) not recover, since McQuirk, as assignor, would only be held liable
    (D) not recover, since Moore remains liable

43. For the purposes of this question only, assume that the original leasehold agreement provided for the rental of the three story house in addition to a two and half-acre tract upon which the house was located. During Moore's tenancy, the State Highway Authority filed proceedings to condemn two acres of the tract for the purpose of highway construction. As a result, Moore contacted Davis and informed him that he should be entitled to an apportioned reduction in the rental. After Davis refused to reduce the rent, Moore brings an action to have his rent apportioned *pro tanto*. Judgment for

    (A) Davis, although Moore would be entitled to terminate the lease
    (B) Davis, since Moore would be held to the original leasehold contract
    (C) Moore, since the value of his leasehold interest was reduced *pro tanto*
    (D) Moore, since eminent domain operates as an apportionment of rent

Questions 44–46 are based on the following fact situation.

Landley owned a large building in the city of Ames. On January 15, 1979, Landley leased the building to Tennance for a period of 20 years at a rental of $10,000 per month. The leasehold agreement between Landley and Tennance provided that the latter was not permitted "to assign this lease to anyone except a corporation with an 'A' credit rating from the Delmarva Credit Rating Corporation." On February 1, 1980, Tennance leased the premises to Aruba Inc., a corporation which did not have the required credit rating. The Tennance-Aruba lease was for a period of five years, with a rental of $15,000 per month, payable by Aruba to Tennance. In addition, Aruba agreed to abide "by all of the terms and conditions of the lease between Landley and Tennance."

One year later, Aruba Inc. leased the premises to Simon for the balance of the term of the Aruba-Tennance lease. Simon took possession of the said premises on February 1, 1981, the same day that Aruba Inc. vacated its occupancy. Pursuant to the Aruba-Simon leasehold agreement, the latter was obligated to pay a monthly rental of $17,500 directly to Aruba Inc. Simon has a 'B' credit rating with the Delmarva Credit Rating Corporation. For one year, Simon paid $17,500 each month directly to Aruba Inc. During that same period, Aruba Inc. continued to pay $15,000 each month to Tennance, while the latter paid $10,000 (each month) to Landley. Landley knew about the leases to Aruba Inc. and Simon, and protested promptly, but took no further action, apparently satisfied as long as he received his $10,000 per month from Tennance.

On February 1, 1982, Simon abandoned the premises and stopped paying rent to Aruba Inc. After Simon discontinued paying rent, Aruba Inc. stopped paying rent to Tennance. When Tennance failed to receive his rent, he, too, stopped paying rent to Landley.

The building is now vacant, and Tennance refuses to pay rent until the air conditioning is fixed. Simon has returned his keys to Aruba Inc., and the latter has returned its keys to Tennance. However, Tennance has not returned any keys to Landley yet. Simon's abandonment was caused by the destruction of the air conditioning unit in a fire apparently set by some vandals. The damaged unit was located in an area inside the store that was used for storing merchandise.

Simon has flatly refused to repair or replace the equipment at his own expense. Despite Simon's repeated demands, Aruba, Tennance, and Landley have all refused to replace the air conditioning system.

44. Which of the following accurately states the legal effect of the non-assignability clause contained in the Landley-Tennance leasehold contract?

(A) The non-assignability provision had no legal effect.
(B) The non-assignability provision made the assignment from Tennance to Aruba ineffective.
(C) The Tennance-Aruba lease did not effectuate a breach of the Landley-Tennance contract.
(D) Although the Tennance-Aruba lease constituted a breach of the Landley-Tennance contract, Landley would nevertheless be required to recognize the validity of the transfer (of the premises) to Aruba.

45. If Landley brings suit to recover for past rent due, which of the following is (are) correct?

   I. Landley may recover against Tennance for past rent due.
   II. Landley may recover against Aruba for past rent due.
   III. Landley may recover against Simon for past rent due.

(A) I only
(B) I and II
(C) II only
(D) I, II, and III

46. Which of the following accurately states the legal relationship(s) of the various parties?

    I. Privity of estate and privity of contract exist between Landley and Tennance.
    II. Privity of estate and privity of contract exist between Tennance and Aruba.
    III. Privity of estate but not privity of contract exists between Landley and Aruba.
    IV. Neither privity of estate nor privity of contract exists between Landley and Simon.

    (A) I and II, but not III and IV
    (B) II and III, but not I and IV
    (C) I and IV, but not II and III
    (D) I, II, and IV, but not III

Question 47 is based on the following fact situation.

Cornell was the owner of a vacant warehouse located in the township of Richmond. On May 1, Cornell leased the warehouse to Yale for a term of five years with a renewable option. The leasehold agreement provided in part:

> "Yale hereby acknowledges that certain areas of the leased premises are in a state of disrepair and unsafe for the conduct of business. Nonetheless, Yale agrees to assume full responsibility for the necessary repairs. Furthermore, Yale agrees to indemnify Cornell for any loss resulting from the condition of the said premises."

Under the terms of the lease, Cornell delivered possession of the warehouse to Yale on May 2. On that date, Brown, who was an employee of Yale's, was working in the warehouse. He was moving some equipment into the warehouse when a section of the ceiling collapsed and fell on him. At the time Cornell and Yale entered into their lease, only Cornell was aware that the ceiling was defective and needed to be repaired. Although Cornell could have remedied the defect before delivering possession to Yale, he (Cornell) didn't perform any repair work on the ceiling. Brown initiated suit against Cornell to recover damages resulting from his injury. There are no applicable statutes.

47. If Brown prevails it will be because a

    (A) landowner is strictly liable for injuries occurring on his property
    (B) landowner's duty of care to third parties cannot be shifted to a tenant by the terms of a lease
    (C) tenant cannot waive the implied warranty of commercial habitability
    (D) covenant to indemnify by a tenant in favor of a landowner is against public policy

Questions 48–50 are based on the following fact situation.

Woody, a famous environmentalist in the State of Sylvania, was the owner of Pocono Woods, a large tract of virgin forest. In 1980, Woody conveyed Pocono Woods "to the people of the State of Sylvania in fee simple; provided, however, that if any portion of said tract shall ever be used or developed for any commercial purpose or otherwise converted from its natural state (with exception for recreational, scientific, or educational purposes), then the grantor or his successors in interest may re-enter as of the grantor's former estate."

Under Sylvania law, conveyances of real property to "the people" of the State are deemed to vest title in the State regarded as a legal entity, and custody over such property resides in an appointed official known as the Director of Environmental Resources. In 1990, the Director granted Crockett Company the privilege to cut timber on a remote portion of Pocono Woods, together with incidental easements of way. The section that Crockett Co. was to clear would be used for the development of a state recreational area.

After the privilege was granted, Crockett proceeded to clear the timber which he later sold for $10,000. When Woody learned that Crockett was cutting the timber and selling it, he notified the Director to desist further exploitation of the land.

48. In 1980, the interest of the State of Sylvania in Pocono Woods would be best described as a

   (A) fee simple determinable
   (B) fee simple subject to condition subsequent
   (C) easement appurtenant
   (D) determinable fee subject to an executory interest

49. The right of Crockett to cut and sell the timber which was to be cleared from Pocono Woods would be an example of a (an)

   (A) license
   (B) easement appurtenant
   (C) easement in gross
   (D) profit-a-prendre

50. In an ejectment action instituted by Woody in 1991 against the State of Sylvania to recover Pocono Woods, what result?

   (A) Woody would succeed, since Crockett's selling of the timber would entitle Woody to re-enter and terminate the grant to the State.
   (B) Woody would succeed, since Crockett's selling of the timber would constitute an automatic termination of the State's fee in Pocono Woods.
   (C) Woody would not succeed, since the Director approved the clearing of the timber in order to develop the area for recreational purposes.
   (D) Woody would not succeed, since the reservation of Woody's right to terminate would be violative of the Rule Against Perpetuities.

Questions 51–53 are based on the following fact situation.

O was the owner of Greenacre in fee simple. A took possession of the land in 1945 as an adverse possessor and remained on the land from 1945 to 1955; he then left the property to care for his sick mother for one year, returning the following year, 1957. Meanwhile, during A's possession O devised Greenacre to B, his son, in 1961. A remained on the property until the present (1977).

Assume that the statutory period for adverse possession in this state is twenty-years.

51. In 1968, O wanted to move back to Greenacre because he desired to return to the country. Finding A in possession, O initiated a suit in ejectment against A. The most probable judicial determination would be

    (A) O would lose, since A's possession was open, hostile, and continuous
    (B) O would lose, because A had fulfilled the required statutory period to become an adverse possessor
    (C) O would win, since A's possession was not continuous
    (D) O would win, because he is the title-holder of record

52. If A's nephew agreed to live and farm the Greenacre property during A's absence, and A then returned from his mother's home in 1957 and thereafter continued in possession until 1968 when O brought the ejectment action, the court would most likely hold that

    (A) O was the rightful owner and thus entitled to possess Greenacre
    (B) O was entitled to possession since A's intermittent possession was insufficient to make him an adverse possessor
    (C) A was entitled to possession because his possession was open, notorious, continuous, and hostile as required for the statutory period
    (D) A was entitled to possession because of the privity between A and his nephew, which aided him in fulfilling the required statutory period

53. Upon O's death in 1977, his sole heir, B, brings an ejectment suit to recover possession of the property from A. In his action, B will most probably

    (A) lose, because A has acquired title by adverse possession
    (B) win, because the statutory period for adverse possession does not run against a remainderman until his interest becomes possessory
    (C) lose, since A was successful in the action by O, B would be estopped from instituting another action against A for ejectment
    (D) win, since his title was perfected at the time of conveyance

Questions 54–55 are based on the following situation.

Judd inherited the bulk of his father's very substantial estate in 1935, including Blackacre, a rambling "farm" of woods and fields in upstate Pennsylvania. Judd, who lived in Philadelphia, used Blackacre as a weekend and holiday retreat. Judd, his wife having predeceased him, died in 1967. His will devised Blackacre to his two sons, Trent and Hunter, "to share and share alike as tenants in common."

At the time of their father's death, Trent lived in Pittsburgh while Hunter resided in Washington, D.C. After Judd's funeral, Trent returned to his residence in Pittsburgh, but Hunter decided to occupy Blackacre. He put his name on the mailbox and has paid the taxes and maintenance expenses. Trent has been generally aware of this, but since he cared little about Blackacre, Trent has never pressed Hunter about the property. Since 1967 Trent has not paid any rent or other compensation to Hunter, nor has Hunter requested such payment.

In January, 1992, a series of disputes arose between Trent and Hunter for the first time concerning their respective rights to Blackacre. The Commonwealth of Pennsylvania recognizes the usual common law types of cotenancies, and there is no applicable legislation on the subject.

54. Hunter brings an appropriate action for the partition of Blackacre by sale and requests that in the division of the proceeds he be awarded an equitable additional amount based on the fact that he paid the taxes and made improvements. If Trent contests the award of this additional sum, judgment for whom?

    (A) Trent, because the maintenance expenses and improvements made by Hunter were voluntary and deemed to have been made for his own convenience
    (B) Trent, because as soon as the maintenance work and improvements were made they became a part of the land owned by the cotenants in equal shares
    (C) Hunter, provided Trent is allowed an equitable setoff for the value of Hunter's occupancy
    (D) Hunter, without any allowance to Trent for a setoff based on the value of Hunter's occupancy

55. Assume for the purposes of this question only that Hunter claims the entire fee simple absolute title to Blackacre and brings an action against Trent to quiet title in himself. If the Commonwealth of Pennsylvania has an ordinary 20 years adverse possession statute, judgment for whom?

    (A) Trent, because one cotenant cannot acquire title by adverse possession against another
    (B) Trent, because there is no evidence that Hunter has performed sufficient acts to constitute an ouster
    (C) Hunter, because the acts of the parties indicate Trent's intention to renounce his ownership rights to Blackacre
    (D) Hunter, because during the past 25 years Hunter has exercised the type of occupancy ordinarily considered sufficient to satisfy adverse possession requirements

Questions 56–58 are based on the following fact situation.

Ash is the owner of record of a parcel of land designated as "A." It is the highest of the three neighboring properties on Big Rock Candy Mountain. Birch is the owner of parcel "B," which is situated lower than "A" on the mountainside. Catskill owns parcel "C," which lies below parcels "A" and "B" on the mountain slope.

In 1980 Ash, who originally owned all three parcels of land, constructed a private drainage system. This system consisted of an underground pipeline which extended across all three parcels of land.

Sewage from parcel "A" drained through the system to a municipal sewer which was located at the bottom of the mountain.

In 1985, Ash sold parcel "B" to Birch. The following year, Catskill purchased parcel "C" from Ash. The deeds to Birch and Catskill did not contain any mention of Ash's drainage system. Located on each of the parcels are large ranch-style homes occupied by the respective owners.

56. Lately, the sewage drain has begun to emit an unpleasant odor across parcel "B." As a result, Birch sued Ash in trespass praying for damages caused by the drainage system. Judgment for

    (A) Ash, since the deed to Birch did not contain any covenants restricting Ash's use of the land
    (B) Ash, since Birch's proper cause of action would be for nuisance, rather than trespass
    (C) Birch, because the drainage system was the proximate cause of plaintiff's damages as a matter of law
    (D) Birch, because Ash did not have the right to improve his own land in a manner which caused harm to another

57. From the standpoint of Birch and Catskill, the drainage system would most likely be defined as a (an)

    (A) easement appurtenant
    (B) easement by implication
    (C) prescriptive easement
    (D) express easement

58. Assume for the purposes of this question only that Catskill's land began to subside over the drainage system. This was because of an especially pliable soil condition of which Ash was unaware prior to construction of the drainage system. In an action brought by Catskill against Ash to recover property damage for the subsidence of his land, judgment for whom?

    (A) Catskill, because Catskill is entitled to lateral support for his land in its natural condition
    (B) Catskill, because Catskill is entitled to subjacent support for his land in its natural condition
    (C) Catskill, because Catskill is entitled to support for his land in its improved condition
    (D) Ash, unless Catskill proves that Ash was negligent in constructing the drainage system

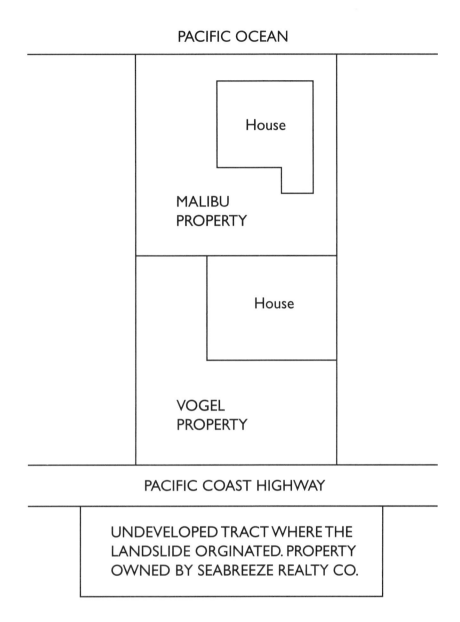

PACIFIC OCEAN

House

MALIBU
PROPERTY

House

VOGEL
PROPERTY

PACIFIC COAST HIGHWAY

UNDEVELOPED TRACT WHERE THE
LANDSLIDE ORGINATED. PROPERTY
OWNED BY SEABREEZE REALTY CO.

Question 59 is based on the following fact situation.

The following incident occurred during the heavy rains that battered Southern California in the winter and spring of 1995. On February 12, 1995, a violent storm struck the Los Angeles basin area. Triggered by heavy rains and wind gusts of over 50 mph, a mudslide caused Velma Vogel's house to be swept downhill into a home owned by Marilyn Malibu. After the Vogel home crashed into Malibu's, the mudslide then carried both of them into the ocean.

Undisputed evidence revealed that the mudslide started when a large plot of land, situated on an uphill slope, owned by the Seabreeze Realty Co., slid downward across Pacific Coast Highway towards the ocean. The landslide then caused the Vogel dwelling to dislodge, rotate, and press against the home of her neighbor, Marilyn Malibu, and both homes then slid into the sea.

59. Malibu asserts a claim against Vogel to recover damages to her home caused by the mudslide. Judgment for whom?

    (A) Malibu, because a landowner has the absolute right to have his land supported laterally by the neighboring land
    (B) Malibu, because one who withdraws lateral support from his neighbor's land is liable for the injury done to such land in its natural condition, regardless of negligence
    (C) Vogel, because although Malibu may recover for injury to the land in its natural condition, she cannot recover for injury to the artificial structures thereon
    (D) Vogel, because Malibu's proper cause of action should be against Seabreeze Realty Co.

Question 60 is based on the following fact situation.

Bobby Saul Estes, a resident of El Paso, had been a Texas state senator for three years. During that period of time, it had been Bobby Saul's regular practice to stay at the Four Seasons Hotel in Austin while the legislature was in session (namely from September through March). As a general rule, Bobby Saul stayed at the hotel each and every night during that seven month period. When Bobby Saul checked into the hotel on September 1, 1997 for the 1997–1998 term, the hotel manager quoted Bobby Saul his usual senatorial discount rate of $50 per night. Although nothing was said regarding payment terms, Bobby Saul customarily paid the bill in weekly installments.

During the months of September and October, he paid the hotel at the end of each week $350 plus tax and other accumulated expenses. On the last day of October, Bobby Saul made his usual weekly payment covering the rental period from October 25th to October 31st. Then on the morning of November 4th (before check-out time for that day), Bobby Saul decided to suddenly move out of the Four Seasons and register into the Ritz Carlton, a new hotel located two blocks away. He notified the manager at the Four Seasons of his intent to check out and tendered a check for $150 plus tax and other incidental charges incurred from November 1st through November 3rd. When the manager noticed that Bobby Saul was only paying for three days, she remarked, "You still owe us $200 plus tax for the rest of the week and $350 plus taxes for an additional week because you didn't give us a week's notice that you planned to vacate." Bobby Saul refused to pay the additional charges.

60. If the Four Seasons Hotel brings suit against Bobby Saul to recover for the unpaid balance, how many additional days lodging will he be required to pay for?

    (A) none
    (B) four
    (C) seven
    (D) eleven

Questions 61–62 are based on the following fact situation.

Jim is the fee simple owner of Blue Bayou, a one-thousand-acre tract of land in Louisiana. Half of Blue Bayou is swampland totally unfit for cultivation, but heavily covered with valuable hardwood timber. The other half of Blue Bayou is also covered with valuable timber, but is land which is fit for the raising of crops when cleared of the timber thereon. The latter section of land is more valuable for cultivation than for the growing of timber.

In 1992, Jim conveyed his Blue Bayou tract to his brother Tim for life. At the time of the conveyance, the swampland had never been used for the production of timber. Tim took possession and cleared forty acres of the timber on the section that was suitable for cultivation. In addition, Tim cut sixty acres of timber in the swampland, thus becoming the first person to exploit this area. He then sold the timber from the swampland for $2,400; he sold the timber from the area adaptable for cultivation for $2,000. Tim then proceeded to clear some timber on the tract and used it as "estovers" for the purpose of utilization in repairing fences, buildings, equipment, and the like on the Blue Bayou property.

61. In an action by Jim to permanently enjoin Tim from cutting any more timber on the swampland section of Blue Bayou and to account for profits received in the sale of the timber, Jim will most likely

    (A) succeed, since a life tenant must account for permissive waste to the reversioner or remainderman
    (B) succeed, since a life tenant may not exploit natural resources where no such prior use had been made
    (C) not succeed, since a life tenant is not liable for ameliorative waste
    (D) not succeed, since a life tenant has a right to make reasonable use of the land.

62. Tim's cutting of the timber on the section of Blue Bayou suitable for cultivation would be an example of

    (A) permissive waste
    (B) ameliorative waste
    (C) equitable waste
    (D) unreasonable exploitation

Question 63 is based on the following fact situation.

Chet Walker died in 1950, owning a tract of land in New Mexico which was then being used for a gold mine, and leaving a will (executed in 1945) in which he specifically devised "my gold mine in New Mexico to my beloved brother, Luke, whatever is left over at his death to go first to his widow if he leaves one and then to his surviving heirs." Chet left the rest and residue of his ample estate in trust for his wife, Wendy, for life, remainder to his son Hal. Chet's only surviving family were Luke, Wendy, and Hal.

Luke continued to mine the land for a number of years, ceasing operations after the profit margin from mining had been destroyed by a combination of increasing costs, diminishing returns, and legal controls on gold prices.

Luke has now acquired some adjacent land which he proposes to use for a mountain resort-hotel. In conjunction with the hotel, he would like to use the tract devised to him by Chet for a riding stable and pasture. This would entail dismantling the mining structures, filling excavations, and constructing the stable buildings. Luke is married and has a 30-year-old son named Wilt, with whom he is not on friendly terms. Wendy and Hal are both still alive. Luke does not want to proceed with redevelopment if there is any significant risk of his being enjoined from continuing.

63. Will anyone be able to obtain an injunction against Luke's proposed redevelopment of the gold mine?

    (A) Yes, because a life tenant or tenant for years is liable to the reversioner or the remainderman for voluntary waste
    (B) Yes, because a life tenant or tenant for years is liable to the reversioner or the remainderman for permissive waste
    (C) Yes, because a life tenant or tenant for years is liable to the reversioner or remainderman for equitable waste
    (D) No, because a life tenant or tenant for years is ordinarily not liable to the reversioner or the remainderman for ameliorating waste

Questions 64–65 are based on the following fact situation.

On May 2, 1992, Abigail Marcus entered into a leasehold agreement for a term of ten years with Ray Haynes, who intended to use Blue Bell Farm for the raising of cattle and hogs. Haynes immediately took possession of the farm and remained in possession as a tenant until November 1, 1999.

Shortly after entering into possession of the farm, Haynes built thereon, at his own expense, a lumber corn crib which was fifteen feet wide and twenty feet long and set on loose bricks. At each corner of the corn crib, he set a wood post in the ground fifteen inches deep and nailed the corn crib to the four corner posts. In 1995, he also built a hog house of brick and mortar on the premises. The hog house was constructed on a cement foundation which extended into the ground twenty-four inches. This structure was twenty feet wide by fifty feet long and was used to keep the brood sows warm during the winter months.

On October 1, 1999, The Farm Life Insurance Co. instituted foreclosure proceedings against Alvin and Abigail Marcus for default of the promissory note on Blue Bell Farm. When Haynes become aware of the foreclosure proceedings, he disengaged the corn crib from the four corner posts (which anchored it in the ground) and removed the corn crib and posts to another farm. Moreover, on October 15, 1999, Haynes dismantled the hog house, brick by brick. He loaded the bricks on his truck and hauled them away.

64. In an action by Abigail Marcus against Ray Haynes alleging waste for removal of certain fixtures (i.e., corn crib and hog house) which of the following is (are) correct?

    I. Haynes would be liable for removal of the corn crib.
    II. Haynes would be liable for removal of the hog house.

    (A) I only
    (B) II only
    (C) I and II
    (D) neither I nor II

65. Assume for the purposes of this question only that The Farm Life Insurance Co. obtained a foreclosure decree against the Marcuses. Both Farm Life Insurance Co. and Abigail Marcus bring separate actions against Ray Haynes alleging waste for removal of trade fixtures. If Farm Life Insurance Co. prevails, it will be because

   (A) Haynes' removal of the corn crib and hog house constituted unpermissive waste
   (B) the claim of the mortgagee would take priority over the claim of the mortgagor to those fixtures which were annexed to the land
   (C) the claim of the mortgagee would take priority over the claim of the mortgagor, only if Haynes was aware of the existence of the mortgage at the time he entered into the leasehold agreement
   (D) the mortgagee would acquire a security interest to the chattel property, even though the latter did not become fixtures

Questions 66–68 are based on the following fact situation.

On January 1, 1979, Barnes entered into an agreement of sale to convey his farm, Winterthur, to Stevens. According to the contract, settlement (or closing) was to take place on March 1, 1979. On January 15, 1979, Stevens conducted a title search on Winterthur and discovered the following transactions in Barnes' chain of title: In 1930, Smith, the record owner of Winterthur, died and in his will he devised Winterthur to "my son, Smitty, and his heirs but if Smitty dies without issue to my daughter, Dixie, and her heirs." The next instrument of record is a deed from Smitty to "Bailey and his heirs" which was executed on July 1, 1940 and recorded on the same date.

In 1941 Bailey died and in his will he devised Winterthur to "my brother Corley for life, then to Corley's heirs." In 1950 Corley executed a general warranty deed in which he conveyed "all my right, title, and interest in Winterthur to my children, Jessie and James." James died intestate in 1955, leaving his son Butch, a four-year-old, as his only heir. Corley died in 1960 leaving Butch and Jessie as heirs.

In 1965 Butch and Jessie conveyed Winterthur by a general warranty deed to "Barnes and his heirs." Although both Butch and Jessie were married, their respectives wives did not join in the deed. Barnes has been in continuous possession of Winterthur since 1965. Smitty died on January 1, 1976 without issue and Dixie is still alive.

66. After Smith's death in 1930, Dixie's interest in Winterthur may best be described as a (an)

   (A) contingent remainder
   (B) springing executory interest
   (C) shifting executory interest
   (D) vested remainder, subject to complete divestiture

67. In March 1976, Dixie, asserting that her title was held free of any claim by Barnes, instituted suit against Barnes to quiet title to Winterthur. Judgment for

   (A) Barnes, since his prior recorded deed would be deemed to be outside Dixie's chain of title
   (B) Barnes, since the devise to Dixie would be violative of the Rule against Perpetuities
   (C) Dixie, since she acquired fee simple interest at the time of Smitty's death in January 1976
   (D) Dixie, since she acquired an indefeasible vested remainder under her father's will in 1930

68. On January 20, 1979, a barn on the Winterthur property was destroyed by fire. When Stevens was notified of the loss the following day, he contacted Barnes and told him that the deal was off because of the fire. As a result, Stevens filed suit against Barnes on January 25, 1979 for a refund of his downpayment of $5,000. In his suit, Stevens will be unsuccessful and will be obliged to complete the contract if the court determines that on January 20th,

   (A) Stevens held the legal title to the farm
   (B) Barnes held the legal title to the farm
   (C) Stevens held the equitable title to the farm
   (D) Barnes held the equitable title to the farm

Question 69 is based on the following fact situation.

Widom is the owner of a large two-story office building in downtown Long Beach. Widom, an architect, designed and supervised the building's construction. He and his associate, Weed, occupy the first floor for their architectural business. On June, 2000, Widom entered into a valid and binding written lease with Coltrane to rent the second floor office space for four years at a monthly rental of $5,000. The lease contained a provision wherein Widom was required to repaint the second floor premises after two years of occupancy.

On June 1, 2002, Coltrane sent Widom a written letter requesting the repainting of the second floor office space. Widom made no reply and failed to perform the repainting as the lease required. The cost of repainting Coltrane's office was estimated at $1,750. On July 1, 2003, Widom had still not repainted the premises. The following day, Coltrane moved out, mailed the keys to Widom, and refused to pay any more rent. The lease was silent as to the rights and remedies of Coltrane due to Widom's failure to perform the repainting. There is no applicable statute in the jurisdiction.

69. In an appropriate action by Widom against Coltrane for the rent due, Widom will

   (A) win, because there was no constructive eviction
   (B) win, because Coltrane had the remedy of self-help
   (C) lose, because he cannot maintain an action for rent while in breach of an express covenant
   (D) lose, because the obligation to pay rent is dependent on Widom's performance of his express covenant

Questions 70–72 are based on the following fact situation.

In a jurisdiction using the grantor/grantee indices, the following events have occurred in the order listed below:

   (1) In 1942, Alpha conveyed to Beta a tract of land now composing Greenacre, by a deed which was immediately recorded.
   (2) In 1962, Beta died a widower and devised Greenacre to his son, Gamma, by a will that was duly admitted to probate.
   (3) In 1973, Gamma mortgaged Greenacre to Epsilon Mortgage Company to secure a note for $25,000, due on December 31, 1983, with 9½% interest per annum.
   (4) In 1976, Epsilon recorded the mortgage on Greenacre.
   (5) In 1983, in a signed writing which Gamma delivered to his daughter, Delta, Gamma promised to convey Greenacre to Delta by a quitclaim deed and pay the mortgage debt when it came due.

70. If Gamma refused to convey Greenacre to Delta and Delta brings suit against Gamma to compel a conveyance of the property, Delta will most likely

    (A) prevail, because there was an effective gift
    (B) prevail, because there was an effective assignment
    (C) not prevail, because there was no consideration to support Gamma's promise to convey the property
    (D) not prevail, because specific performance will not be granted where there is an adequate remedy at law

71. Suppose that Gamma did, in fact, deliver to Delta a quitclaim deed which made no reference to the mortgage. If Gamma thereafter defaulted on the mortgage debt, which of the following is probably correct?

    (A) Only Delta has a cause of action against Gamma.
    (B) Only Epsilon has a cause of action against Gamma.
    (C) Both Delta and Epsilon have causes of action against Gamma.
    (D) Neither Delta nor Epsilon has a cause of action against Gamma.

72. Suppose that Gamma did, in fact, deliver to Delta a quitclaim deed which made no reference to the mortgage. If Gamma thereafter defaulted on the mortgage and Epsilon brought an in personam action against Delta to recover the amount due on the mortgage debt, the mortgagee will probably

    (A) succeed, because Epsilon is a third party beneficiary of the agreement between Gamma and Delta
    (B) succeed, because there was an implied delegation of duties to Delta
    (C) not succeed, because Delta did not promise to pay the mortgage debt
    (D) not succeed, because the law does not permit the mortgagor to delegate duties under this type of a property transfer

Questions 73–74 are based on the following fact situation.

Hancock, the owner of Hancock House Apartments, orally entered into a five-year lease with Jay, with the rental period to commence on February 1, 1978. The lease provided that Jay would pay Hancock rent at the rate of $3,500 per year for a one-bedroom apartment.

Jay made payments of $3,500 on the first day of February in 1978 and 1979. On March 31, 1979, Hancock notified Jay and the other tenants of the apartment building that he had sold the building that day to Madison. The following day, Madison, the new owner, notified Jay that the building would be converted to a condominium and that Jay's lease would be terminated as of December 31, 1979. However, Jay would be entitled to purchase the condominium unit (an interest in real estate subject to recording statutes) at a special resident's discount price of $32,500, if Jay signed an agreement of sale within six months.

Jay decided not to purchase the unit, because he had already planned to move away to the city of Anatevka. However, Fred, who was Jay's friend, wanted to buy Jay's unit at the discounted price. Since Madison would sell to Fred only at the nonresident's price of $38,500, Fred consulted a lawyer and determined how he could purchase at the lower price by a series of transactions.

Jay signed an agreement of sale on May 1, 1979 and purchased the unit at the discounted price. Closing was held on September 15, 1979. On September 16, 1979, Jay conveyed his entire interest to Fred for $32,500. The two deeds were recorded immediately, in proper order.

On July 3, 1980, Fred signed an agreement to sell his interest in the unit to Miss Kitty for $47,500. Closing was scheduled for September 17, 1980.

73. On April 2, 1979, considering all appropriate defenses, the termination date of Jay's lease was

    (A) September 15, 1979
    (B) December 31, 1979
    (C) January 31, 1980
    (D) January 31, 1983

74. If Miss Kitty properly checks the real estate records prior to her closing she would

    (A) look for Fred's name in the grantee index
    (B) look for Fred's name in the grantor index
    (C) look for Fred's name in the grantee and grantor index
    (D) not look for Fred's name in either the grantee or grantor

Questions 75–76 are based on the following fact situation.

Looney was the owner of a 300-acre tract of land that was located in Pittman County. Over the course of time, she developed the property into a residential subdivision known as Devonshire. Lincoln Boulevard, a four-lane public highway, ran along the northern boundary of Devonshire. When Devonshire was first plotted, Looney constructed a private road called Looney Lane across the western boundary of the subdivision. Looney Lane was used only for the benefit of the owners who purchased lots in the subdivision.

Dooley owned a 20-acre tract that was situated just below Lincoln Boulevard and immediately adjacent to the west side of Looney Lane. Dooley's property was divided into two 10-acre parcels: Parcel 1 was the northern half and bordered along Lincoln Boulevard; Parcel 2 was the southern sector and abutted the Peekskill River. In 1997, Dooley conveyed Parcel 1 to Perez by warranty deed. No encumbrances were mentioned in the deed. Six months later, Dooley conveyed Parcel 2 by warranty deed to Eagleson. Both Perez and Eagleson promptly recorded their deeds with the Pittman County Recorder's Office.

75. Assume for the purposes of this question only that no part of Parcel 2 adjoins a public road. Consequently, Eagleson constructed an access road connecting his property to Looney Lane. After Eagleson used Looney Lane for approximately two months, Slotnick, a Devonshire lot owner, ordered Eagleson to discontinue using the private road. In an appropriate action by Slotnick against Eagleson to enjoin the use of Looney Lane, Eagleson will

    (A) win, because there is an easement by necessity over Looney Lane
    (B) win, because there is an implied easement appurtenant over Looney Lane
    (C) lose, unless Looney Lane is the only access road by which Eagleson can gain ingress and egress to his property
    (D) lose, because he has no legal right to travel over Looney Lane

76. Assume the following facts for this question only. In 1965, Dooley constructed a driveway from Looney Lane over what is now Parcel 2. This driveway, which extended over Parcel 1 where it connected with Lincoln Boulevard, was used continuously by Dooley until 1997 when he conveyed his property to Perez and Eagleson. When Eagleson took possession of Parcel 2, he immediately began to use the driveway across Parcel 1. Thereafter, Perez requested that Eagleson cease to use the driveway over Parcel 1. After Eagleson refused, Perez brought an appropriate action to enjoin Eagleson from using the driveway. In this action, Perez will

    (A) win, because his deed antedated Eagleson's deed
    (B) win, because no encumbrances were mentioned in his deed
    (C) lose, because Eagleson has an easement by necessity
    (D) lose, because Eagleson has a prescriptive easement

Question 77 is based on the following fact situation.

Carson is the owner of a parcel of land known as Tall Acres, which is situated upon the top of Candy Rock Mountain. Located below Tall Acres is Grasslands, a forty-acre hillside estate which is owned by DuVall. Crystal Stream is a non-navigable watercourse that originates at the top of Candy Rock Mountain and runs all the way down into the San Vicente Valley. Both Tall Acres and Grasslands are within the watershed of Crystal Stream.

When DuVall purchased Grasslands in 1980, he started taking water from Crystal Stream and used it to irrigate the southern half of his property, which he has used as a farm. Prior to 1980, the southern half of Grasslands had been cleared and placed in cultivation, while the northern half remained wooded and unused except for an occasional hike or gathering of timber for use as domestic fuel. DuVall continued this established pattern of use. Now (January, 2002), he is still taking water from Crystal Stream and using it to irrigate the southern half of Grasslands.

In 2000, Carson built a home on Tall Acres and started taking water from Crystal Stream for domestic purposes. During that year there was heavy rainfall, and this caused Crystal Stream to run down the mountain at a high water level. The next year, however, there was a drought. As a result, Crystal Stream flowed at a very low level. Consequently, there was only enough water to irrigate DuVall's farmland or, in the alternative, to supply all of Carson's domestic water needs and one-quarter of DuVall's irrigation requirements. Candy Rock Mountain is located in a jurisdiction where the period of prescription is fifteen years.

77. Inasmuch as Crystal Stream is still flowing at a very low level and Carson is continuing to take water for his personal needs, there is insufficient water to irrigate Grasslands. As a consequence, DuVall brings an appropriate action to declare that his water rights to the stream are superior to those of Carson. In addition, DuVall moves to have the full flow of Crystal Stream passed to him, notwithstanding the effect it might have on Carson. If this state follows the common law of riparian rights but does not follow the doctrine of prior appropriation, judgment for whom?

(A) Carson, because as an upstream landowner, he would have superior rights to the water over a downstream owner
(B) Carson, because domestic use is superior to and is protected against an agricultural use
(C) DuVall, because he has obtained an easement by prescription to remove as much water as he may need
(D) DuVall, because he has put the water to a beneficial use prior to Carson's use and has continuously used the water

Questions 78–79 are based on the following fact situation.

In 1954, Oswald, a devoted conservationist, was the owner of Greenacre, a 100-acre tract of undeveloped land. In that year, Oswald conveyed Greenacre "to Grant in fee simple, provided, however, that the grantee agrees that neither he nor his heirs or assigns shall ever use the property for any commercial purpose." The deed further stipulated that "if any portion of said tract is used for other than residential purposes, then the grantor or his successors in interest may re-enter as of the grantor's former estate." This deed was properly recorded. Grant died intestate in 1972, survived by Wilma, his wife. Oswald died in 1975, survived by his children, Carla and Carrie, his only heirs.

During the period between 1954 and 1980, the spreading development from the nearby city of Greenville has begun to engulf Greenacre. Though still undeveloped, Greenacre has become surrounded by office buildings, shopping malls, and other commercial edification. In 1982, Wilma executed and delivered to Miles a fee simple conveyance of Greenacre, which Miles immediately recorded. The deed did not contain any reference to the restriction noted above. After Miles acquired title to Greenacre, he planned to commence construction of a hotel complex on a portion of the tract that bordered an apartment building. The applicable recording statute in effect in this jurisdiction provides, in part "No deed or other instrument in writing, not recorded in accordance with this statute, shall affect the title or rights to, in any real estate, or any devisee or purchaser in good faith, without knowledge of the existence of such unrecorded instruments."

78. If Carla brings suit to enjoin Miles from constructing the hotel, the plaintiff will most likely

(A) win, because Miles is charged by the recording act with notice of the provision in the original deed
(B) win, because either Carla or Carrie has the right of reentry for condition broken
(C) lose, because the change in the character of the surrounding area has rendered the restriction meaningless
(D) lose, because a common development scheme had been established for the entire Greenacre tract

79. Assume for the purposes of this question only that Grant developed Greenacre into a residential subdivision between 1960 and 1969. The 100-acre tract was divided into single acre lots, all of which were sold during the same decade. Single family residential dwellings were constructed on all of the lots except four, which were sold to Horne in 1968. The deed to the four lots contained the same restriction as stipulated in the Oswald-Grant deed. In 1980, the Federal Savings & Loan Co. acquired Horne's four lots in a foreclosure proceeding, and in the same year sold the property to Holiday. If Holiday seeks to construct a service station on his parcel of land, which of the following arguments, if true, would offer him the best chance of implementation?

(A) The restriction against residential use is void as violative of the Rule Against Perpetuities.

(B) The commercial development surrounding the property has made the deed restriction unenforceable.

(C) When Holiday purchased the property from Federal Savings & Loan, the deed did not contain any mention of the restriction.

(D) The jurisdiction in which Greenacre is located approved a zoning ordinance permitting the commercial development of the area surrounding Holiday's property.

Question 80 is based on the following fact situation.

Rose, owner of Roseacre, granted to Morgan, owner of Diamondacre, an easement of way. Rose then went to Japan to live. Morgan then moved into possession of Roseacre and used it openly and exclusively, paying the taxes, for 23 years. He did not use his easement during that period. Rose returned and tried to evict Morgan from Roseacre. The court held that Morgan had acquired Roseacre by adverse possession. Morgan then sold Roseacre back to Rose, who then put a chain across the easement. Morgan has now brought an action to remove the chain.

80. In most jurisdictions, Morgan will

(A) lose, because he abandoned his easement

(B) lose, because he did not use his easement for the statutory period of 20 years

(C) lose, because, rather than using his easement, he used all of Roseacre

(D) win, because mere non-use of an easement does not extinguish it

Questions 81–82 are based on the following fact situation.

R.J. Longhorn was a cattle rancher who owned substantial oil and mineral interests in West Texas. In July, 1990, Longhorn acquired title to Alpine Flats, a 200-acre tract located just inside the city limits of El Paso. The property was purchased at a sheriff's sale after its former owner, N.E. Fectual, became delinquent on his property taxes.

In 1997, Longhorn decided to relocate in California and sell his vast ranching and oil interests in the Southwest. In July, Longhorn conveyed Alpine Flats for a consideration of $1.00, receipt of which was acknowledged, "to Austin, his heirs, and assigns, but if Austin's wife, Molly, dies without issue, to Rosalina and her heirs and assigns."

After taking possession of Alpine Flats, Austin discovered considerable oil reserves on the property. He thus began oil drilling operations and removed large quantities of oil which he sold on the spot market. At no time did he give notice to Rosalina of his oil drilling activities. Months passed before Rosalina learned that Austin was selling oil from the drilling operations.

81. Rosalina has now brought an action in equity for an accounting of the value of the oil removed and for an injunction against any further oil removal. If the decision is in favor of Austin, it will be on account of the fact that

    (A) the right to remove oil is an incident of a defeasible fee simple
    (B) Rosalina has no interest in Alpine Flats
    (C) there was no showing that Austin acted in bad faith
    (D) the right to remove oil is an incident of the right to possession

82. If Molly died without issue before the beginning of Austin's oil drilling operations, the likelihood of Rosalina's success in her lawsuit against Austin would probably have been

    (A) unaffected, because the right to remove oil is an incident of the right to possession
    (B) unaffected, because the nature of Austin's estate would not be altered by Molly's death
    (C) improved, because Molly's death without issue would convert Austin's fee into a reversionary interest
    (D) improved, because although Austin still has a fee, it would now be certain to terminate

Question 83 is based on the following fact situation.

Erickson owned Hillacre, a ten-acre tract of land, in fee simple. Hillacre was located in the township of Deer Valley. In 1968, Erickson conveyed Hillacre to The Downhill Development Association "on condition that a ski lodge and resort area be built thereon and the land be used solely for skiing purposes and, in the event that said property is not used as a ski resort, the property shall revert to myself, the grantor, my heirs, or assigns." Subsequently, a ski lodge was built and the land was continuously used as a ski resort for over twenty years.

In 1978, Stein, owner of Grassacre, a property abutting the northeast corner of Hillacre, began to use a portion of Hillacre in order to gain access to Grassacre for ingress and egress. He used this access road openly, visibly, and notoriously until 1999. The period of prescription in this particular jurisdiction was 20 years. In March, 2000, he decided to sell Grassacre to Grich for the purchase price of $500,000. Thereupon, Stein and Grich entered into a written real estate sales contract with closing being set for May 1, 2000.

On April 1, 2000, Downer, the president of The Downhill Development Association, was approached by Grich with the request that written easement be given over the access road and that an appropriate instrument be delivered to Grich concurrently with Grich's closing with Stein. Following Downer's meeting with Grich, The Downhill Development Association held a duly announced meeting and voted unanimously to authorize its trustees to grant such an easement.

On April 15, 2000, Erickson died. Erickson's sole descendant and successor in interest was his wife, Erika. Upon her husband's death, she immediately notified The Downhill Development Association that if it granted the easement to Grich, Hillacre would revert to her. Grich then brought an appropriate action, joining Stein, Erika and The Downhill Development Association, seeking a declaratory judgment that Stein has a perpetual easement appurtenant to Hillacre.

83. In this action, judgment should be in favor of which of the following parties?

(A) Erika, because Grich could not obtain rights against The Downhill Development Association by prescription

(B) Erika, because the easement would violate the negative restriction that Erickson originally sought to impose

(C) Grich, because Stein had already obtained an easement by prescription

(D) Grich, because the language of the conveyance to The Downhill Development Association was too vague to support any claim by Erika

Questions 84–87 are based on the following fact situation.

In 1850 the State of Baden conveyed to Evers a tract of land, which today composes the two farms of Breezyacre and Windyacre, by deed that was immediately recorded. Evers died a widower in 1900, devising all of his real property to his son Warner. The will was duly probated shortly thereafter.

In 1915, Warner conveyed the Breezyacre-Windyacre tract to Tidwell. This deed was not recorded until after Warner's death in 1919. Warner's will, duly probated following his death, named Tidwell as sole legatee and devisee of Warner's entire estate.

In 1918, Warner mortgaged the Breezyacre-Windyacre tract to the Baden National Bank. The mortgage instrument, which was recorded in 1918, recited that it was subordinate to a mortgage on the same land given by Warner to Miller in 1898 and recorded in 1898. In that instrument Warner purported to grant Miller a mortgage on the Breezyacre-Windyacre tract.

In 1941, Tidwell conveyed the parcel known as Breezyacre to Rumson, retaining Windyacre. This deed was duly recorded, but did not mention any mortgage.

In 1956, Rumson conveyed Breezyacre to Vincent, who promptly recorded the deed. Recorded at the same time was an instrument from the Baden National Bank discharging and releasing the 1918 mortgage, which recited that the underlying debt had been fully repaid.

In 1970, Baggett entered into an agreement with Vincent, whereby Vincent would convey Breezyacre in fee simple to Baggett for the sum of $75,000. The closing date was set for January 15,1971.

NOTE that all of the deeds mentioned in the aforementioned transactions are general warranty deeds. In addition, the State of Baden has a notice-type recording statute and follows a title theory for mortgages.

84. In 1915, asserting that his title to the Breezyacre-Windyacre tract was held free of any claim by Miller, Tidwell instituted suit against Miller to quiet title to the property. Judgment for

    (A) Tidwell, since Warner did not own the property in 1898, and therefore, his mortgage to Miller would be ineffective
    (B) Tidwell, since a subsequent bona fide purchaser without notice would prevail over a prior mortgagee
    (C) Miller, since under the after acquired title doctrine, where the mortgagor mortgages a larger estate than he possesses in the land and subsequently acquires such larger estate, it inures to the benefit of the mortgagee
    (D) Miller, since in the title theory state, a mortgagee would prevail over a bona fide purchaser

85. What is the probable legal effect of Warner's mortgage (agreement) in 1918 with the Baden National Bank?

    (A) The mortgage would be invalid, since Warner conveyed his interest in the property to Tidwell in 1915.
    (B) The mortgage would be invalid, since the first mortgage in 1898 would take precedence over the second mortgage.
    (C) The mortgage would be invalid, unless the mortgagee Baden National Bank had knowledge of the prior conveyance to Tidwell.
    (D) The subsequent mortgagee, Baden National Bank, would prevail as against the prior conveyee-Tidwell, who failed to record before the mortgage was effectuated.

86. Assume that on January 10, 1971, Baggett conducted a title search which revealed the existence of Miller's 1898 mortgage on the Breezyacre-Windyacre tract. Which of the following statements is most accurate with respect to that mortgage?

    (A) Baggett would be entitled to rescind the real estate contract with Vincent immediately.
    (B) The encumbrance renders title to Breezyacre unmarketable.
    (C) The mortgage would only encumber the Windyacre parcel, not the Breezyacre tract, since Tidwell's partition in 1941 created a joint tenancy.
    (D) The encumbrance would not entitle Baggett to rescind the real estate contract until closing on January 15th.

87. Assume for the purposes of this question only that on January 15,1971, the sale of Breezyacre is finalized, with Baggett paying Vincent $75,000 and Vincent executing a general warranty deed. The deed contains the following covenants of title:

    (a) Covenant for seisin;
    (b) Covenant of the right to convey; and
    (c) Covenant against encumbrances.

After Baggett takes possession of Breezyacre, he learns of the Warner-Miller 1898 mortgage, which was not satisfied, and seeks monetary damages for breach of the covenant against encumbrances. Judgment for

- (A) Baggett, since the covenant against encumbrances is a guarantee to the grantee that the property is not subject to outstanding rights or interests
- (B) Baggett, since the covenant against encumbrances would be breached at the time the deed was delivered, thereby entitling the covenantee to recover damages
- (C) Vincent, since the covenant against encumbrances may only be breached, if at all, at the time of conveyance
- (D) Vincent, unless the covenantee is disturbed in his actual enjoyment of the land thereby conveyed

Question 88 is based on the following fact situation.

Amos is the owner in fee simple of Blackacre, a seven-acre tract, on which he maintains a dwelling house for himself and his family. Adjoining Blackacre is Whiteacre, a 10-acre tract, owned by Andy. In order to gain access to the highway, Amos has an easement to cross over Whiteacre.

Amos has recently purchased Greenacre, a 12-acre tract, which abuts Whiteacre but is not appurtenant to Blackacre. Amos has begun constructing a farmhouse on Greenacre and is using the existing easement (across Whiteacre) to gain access to the 12-acre tract. Amos has never received permission from Andy to use the road across Whiteacre to gain access to Greenacre.

88. In an appropriate action by Andy to enjoin Amos from using the existing easement to gain access to Greenacre, the plaintiff will most likely

- (A) succeed, because Amos is making use of the servient tenement beyond the scope and extent of the easement as it was originally created
- (B) succeed, because Amos has no right to use the servient tenement in connection with a tract of land which is not part of the dominant tenement
- (C) not succeed, because Amos has an easement by necessity
- (D) not succeed, because Amos has a right to use the easement in a manner not inconsistent with the rights of the owner of the servient tenement

Question 89 is based on the following fact situation.

Mays owns Whiteacre, a 10-acre tract used for agricultural purposes, in fee simple. On Whiteacre Mays maintains a dwelling house for himself and his family. Mantle is the fee simple owner of Blackacre, a five-acre tract, which abuts Whiteacre. In 1964 Mays began to erect a concrete wall along the boundary line appurtenant to Blackacre. After Mays started to build the wall, Mantle informed him that he believed the wall was protruding onto his property. Mays informed Mantle that he paid $500 to have the boundary line surveyed. Mays said that the surveyor indicated that the wall did not encroach on Blackacre. Mantle accepted Mays' assurances and in 1980 devised Blackacre to Snider.

After Snider entered into possession of Blackacre, he had the boundary line surveyed. The survey conclusively showed that the concrete wall extended two feet onto Blackacre. Although the encroachment does not interfere with Snider's use of Blackacre, he nevertheless demanded that Mays remove the wall. Upon Mays' refusal, Snider brought an appropriate action to have the wall removed.

89. The most likely result is that

(A) Mays must remove the wall at his own expense
(B) Mays must remove the wall but at Snider's expense
(C) Mays may leave the wall without being liable to Snider for money damages
(D) Mays may leave the wall but he will be liable to Snider for money damages

Question 90 is based on the following fact situation.

Bradley was the record owner in fee simple absolute of Greenacre, a 125-acre parcel of land located in Oxford. In 1998 Bradley conveyed the property "to my sister, Martina, for life with remainder to my son, Reed, if he be living." At the time of the conveyance, Reed was in medical school in Grenada. Martina immediately recorded the deed and took possession.

Shortly thereafter, Martina discovered that the property contained large coal deposits which she severed and began to sell. In 2001 Reed graduated from medical school and returned to Oxford. He then learned of the conveyance and also ascertained that Martina had not paid taxes on Greenacre for the last three years. After discovering that the property was subject to a pending tax foreclosure, Reed demanded that Martina pay the delinquent taxes. Even though the profits from the coal sales were quite substantial, Martina refused to pay the outstanding taxes. Reed thus paid the taxes himself.

90. If Reed sues Martina to recover the taxes and for an accounting of the proceeds received from the coal sales, judgment should be

(A) in favor of Reed for the taxes but not for the coal
(B) in favor of Reed for the coal but not for the taxes
(C) in favor of Reed for both the taxes and the coal
(D) against Reed for both the taxes and the coal

Questions 91–93 are based on the following fact situation.

In August 1953, Oscar, who was the owner of 1500 acres of undeveloped timberland, mortgaged his land to Jackson by a mortgage deed, which was not recorded in the Tract Index until January 1954. The mortgage was given to secure a note for $50,000, repayable over a twenty-year period.

In September 1953, Oscar executed a warranty deed purporting to convey the same land to Babson in fee simple. Babson recorded immediately in the Grantor-Grantee Index. Then in April 1954, Babson conveyed the same tract to Callahan in fee simple by warranty deed. Callahan paid full market value and recorded the deed at once in the Grantor-Grantee Index.

The land in question had never been occupied, fenced, or cleared except that between the years 1950–1974, Groves Mining Co., owner of an adjacent tract, regularly drove trucks over a cleared path pursuant to a 1950 agreement with Oscar. The agreement, which was duly recorded, provided that "the parties expressly agree and Oscar promises that Oscar and his successors shall refrain from obstructing the said described pathway across Oscar's land which the Groves Mining Co. and its successors may perpetually use as a road, in consideration of which Groves, and its successors, will pay the sum of $700 per annum."

During the period between 1954 through 1975, Callahan collected the yearly $700 fees from Groves and also paid all property taxes.

In November 1977, Callahan entered into a contract to sell the land to Daniels. The contract called for a "good and marketable title" with an express exception for rights under the 1950 Oscar Groves agreement. However, Daniels learned about the 1953 mortgage in the course of his title search and refused to honor the contract for sale of the property.

Assume this jurisdiction follows a lien theory for mortgages and has a pure-notice type recording statute.

91. Asserting that he had marketable title, Callahan instituted suit against Daniels for specific performance. If Callahan prevails, it will be because

    (A) Callahan's grantor, Babson, recorded before Jackson
    (B) Jackson's prior recorded mortgage is deemed to be outside Callahan's chain of title
    (C) Callahan's grantor, Babson, had no notice of Jackson's mortgage interest
    (D) as between two warranty deeds, the latter one is controlling

92. The provision in the 1950 agreement between Oscar and Groves Mining Co. granting "the use of the pathway" to Groves may best be described as a (an)

    (A) license
    (B) easement in gross
    (C) easement appurtenant
    (D) prescriptive easement

93. Assume for the purposes of this question only that in 1954, after the conveyance from Babson, Callahan informed Groves Mining Co., that he would no longer honor the 1950 agreement permitting Groves to use the pathway. Groves brought an action for specific performance. Judgment for

    (A) Groves, since their property interest would "run with the land"
    (B) Groves, since the possessor of a servient interest would prevail against subsequent owners
    (C) Callahan, since Groves' interest was extinguished by the subsequent conveyance
    (D) Callahan, since there was no privity of estate between Callahan and Groves

Questions 94–95 are based on the following fact situation.

In 1999, Johnson conveyed 100 acres of his Red Oak farm in Dallas County to Williams. The deed contained the following covenants: (1) seisin, (2) right to convey, and (3) against encumbrances. Subsequently, Williams conveyed the property to Allen by warranty deed. However, Allen is later evicted by Davidson because of paramount title.

94. Allen now brings suit against Johnson for breach of covenants in the deed. Judgment should be for

    (A) Allen, because the covenants contained in the deed run with the land
    (B) Johnson, since no privity of estate exists between Allen and him
    (C) Allen, but only for the covenants of seisin and right to convey
    (D) Johnson, because the covenants are personal in nature and do not run with the land

95. For the purposes of this question only, suppose that Johnson conveyed the property to Williams and there was an outstanding mortgage. The deed contained the above-mentioned covenants. Williams took possession, and shortly thereafter, threatened with foreclosure, he paid off the mortgage with interest. Williams now sues for breach of covenant against encumbrances. The court will most likely allow recovery for

    (A) the amount in principal and in interest thereon from the time of the mortgage payment
    (B) only the principal which Williams paid on the mortgage
    (C) the measure of value between the value of the land with and without such an encumbrance
    (D) no recovery, since Williams should have brought suit against Johnson immediately upon notice of the outstanding mortgage

Questions 96–98 are based on the following fact situation.

Scenicacre is a twenty-acre tract of open meadowland with numerous streams running through. In 1965 Ohner had good record title to Scenicacre in fee simple absolute. In 1966 Ohner delivered to Son, with intent to make a gift of Scenicacre to Son, a deed signed by Ohner, naming Son and his heirs grantee and appearing valid on its face. Son neglected to record the deed.

In 1970, Buyer, aware of the existence of the Ohner-to-Son deed, sought out Ohner and asked to buy for $10,000 a deed of Scenicacre from Ohner to Buyer and his heirs. Ohner executed such a deed and Buyer promptly recorded it. Buyer's intent was to acquire color of title and obtain ownership of Scenicacre by adverse possession. In 1970, Buyer constructed a fence around Scenicacre.

In 1971, Son presented his deed of Scenicacre to Purchaser and, for $15,000 paid by Purchaser, signed and delivered a deed of Scenicacre in favor of Purchaser and his heirs. After receiving the deed, Purchaser made no effort to search the title, to examine the property, or to record the deed.

In 1975, Vendee paid Buyer $20,000 and Buyer delivered to Vendee a deed of Scenicacre in favor of Vendee and his heirs. Vendee had examined the property, had searched the title, and had no knowledge of Buyer's awareness of the prior Ohner-to-Son instrument. Although Vendee did not reside on the property, he regularly visited Scenicacre twice a week. Vendee recorded his deed.

In 1979 for $25,000 paid by Oscar, Purchaser signed and delivered a deed of Scenicacre naming Oscar and his heirs as grantees. Oscar obtained from Purchaser the Son-to-Purchaser deed, and from Son the Ohner-to-Son deed and took all three documents to the Recorder's Office to be recorded. At Oscar's request, all three instruments were recorded in the following order: (1) Ohner-to-Son; (2) Son-to-Purchaser; (3) Purchaser-to-Oscar.

Before Oscar had paid Purchaser and taken his deed, Oscar visited Scenicacre and observed the fence. However, Vendee was not present when Oscar visited the property and nothing suggested who, if anyone, was using it. In any case, Oscar did not attempt to search the title before making his purchase. NOTE: This jurisdiction uses Grantor-Grantee Indices and has no Tract Index.

96. In 1980, what is the present state of title to Scenicacre if the jurisdiction's recording act provides "Every conveyance of real property shall be invalid as against any person, except the grantor, his heirs, and assigns, having actual notice thereof, unless it is recorded as provided by Statute"?

    (A) In a notice jurisdiction, Oscar, as a subsequent bona fide purchaser, is only chargeable with notice of what appears in his chain of title and therefore would acquire record title to Scenicacre.
    (B) In a race-notice jurisdiction, Buyer would acquire equitable title to Scenicacre, since he erected the fence and failed to inform Vendee of the prior Ohner-to-Son instrument.
    (C) In a race-notice jurisdiction, Vendee, as subsequent bona fide purchaser without notice of prior Ohner-to-Son instrument, would acquire record title to Scenicacre.
    (D) In a notice jurisdiction, purchaser would acquire record title to Scenicacre even though he failed to record his deed.

97. In 1980, what is the present state of title to Scenicacre if the jurisdiction's recording act provides "Every conveyance of real estate which is not recorded is void against a subsequent purchaser in good faith for valuable consideration, whose conveyance shall be first duly recorded"?

    (A) In a race-notice jurisdiction, Oscar, as a subsequent bona fide purchaser, would acquire record title to Scenicacre, since he was the last in time to record.
    (B) In a pure race jurisdiction, Buyer would acquire record title to Scenicacre, since he purchased the property for value and recorded first in time.
    (C) In a race-notice jurisdiction, Vendee, as a subsequent bona fide purchaser without notice of the prior Ohner-to-Son instrument, would acquire record title to Scenicacre, since he recorded his deed first in time.
    (D) In a pure race jurisdiction, Vendee, as a subsequent bona fide purchaser without notice of the prior Ohner-to-Son instrument, would acquire record title to Scenicacre, since he recorded his deed first in time.

98. Assume for the purposes of this question only, that (in question 97), when Vendee purchased Scenicacre from Buyer in 1975, he was aware of the Ohner-to-Son instrument. In 1980, in an action to quiet title to Scenicacre, which of the following parties would have priority of title?

    (A) Oscar
    (B) Buyer
    (C) Vendee
    (D) Purchaser

Question 99 is based on the following fact situation.

Anderson owned Hillcrest, a seventy-acre tract located in Coatsville. In 1989, Anderson sold fifteen acres of Hillcrest to Barrington. The deed of conveyance contained the following clause:

"The parties hereby covenant that if the grantor, Anderson, proposes to sell any or all of the remaining fifty-five acres of Hillcrest during Barrington's lifetime, then the grantee, Barrington, shall have the right of first refusal to purchase said parcel on the same terms and conditions as proposed; and, in the alternative, if grantee , Barrington, proposes to sell any or all of the fifteen acres of his parcel during Anderson's lifetime, then Anderson shall have the reciprocal right of first refusal."

In December, 1997, Barrington was approached by Carper who offered to purchase his fifteen-acre parcel for $100,000. Barrington did not afford Anderson an opportunity to exercise his right of first refusal, and he went ahead and sold the property to Carper. After Carper took possession, Anderson then learned about the sale. Anderson immediately brought suit against Barrington and Carper to enforce the right of first refusal in the deed.

99. Based on the facts as presented, Anderson will

    (A) win, because Barrington has a reciprocal right of first refusal
    (B) win, because Anderson's right of first refusal does not violate the Rule Against Perpetuities since it is limited to his lifetime
    (C) lose, because the rights of first refusal are unreasonable restraints on alienation
    (D) lose, because the rights of first refusal only relate to land that is not conveyed by deed

Question 100 is based on the following fact situation.

Winslow was the record title owner in fee simple absolute of Blackacre, a 100-acre tract of farmland located in the township of Devonshire. In 1990, Winslow devised the property to his daughters, Amy and Brooke, as joint tenants with right of survivorship. The next year, Amy executed a deed to Cooke as follows:

> "I hereby convey all of my right, title, and interest in the North East Quarter of Blackacre to Cooke and his heirs."

Thereafter, Amy borrowed $100,000 from Drake and a promissory note was executed as evidence of the debt. In 2000, Amy defaulted on the loan and Drake, as judgment creditor, levied upon and sold to Zorn on execution sale all of "Amy's right, title, and interest in the South Half of Blackacre." In December, 2001, Amy died intestate leaving Hilton, her husband, as her sole surviving heir.

100. Who owns Blackacre?

(A) Brooke and Cooke are tenants in common of the North East Quarter of Blackacre; Brooke and Hilton are tenants in common of the North West Quarter of Blackacre; and Brook and Zorn are tenants in common of the South Half of Blackacre.

(B) Brooke and Cooke are tenants in common of the North East Quarter of Blackacre; Brooke is the owner in fee of the North West Quarter of Blackacre; and Brooke and Zorn are tenants in common of the South Half of Blackacre.

(C) Brooke and Cooke are tenants in common of the North East Quarter of Blackacre; Brooke and Hilton are tenants in common of the North West Quarter of Blackacre; and Zorn is the owner in fee of the south Half of Blackacre.

(D) Brooke and Cooke are tenants in common of the North East Quarter of Blackacre; and Brooke is the owner in fee of the remaining three-quarters of Blackacre.

1. **(D)** In order for a covenant to run with the land, four elements must co-exist: (1) there must be a writing; (2) there must be an intention that the covenant run with the land; (3) the covenant must "touch and concern" the land; and (4) there must be privity of estate. In the present example, no privity of estate exists between Wilkes and the Lovette Preservation League. As a consequence, provision (a) cannot be viewed as a covenant running with the land. By process of elimination, choice (D) is therefore the best answer.

2. **(A)** Section (b) of the Wilkes-Lovette agreement would be construed as an easement. An easement is the right of one person to go onto the land in possession of another and make a limited use thereof.

3. **(B)** A "fee" describes a freehold estate of inheritance which has potentially infinite duration, or which can be terminable upon the happening of an event (i.e., "defeasance"). As a possessory real property interest, a defeasible fee can be distinguished from a covenant, choice (C), or an equitable servitude, choice (A). The latter two interests are *non-possessory* interests which act as private land use restrictions. Since Duffy wants to transfer *ownership* of the island to Dawn, he must convey to her a possessory interest. Choice (B), a defeasible fee, is the correct answer, since it is the only possessory interest given. Choice (D) is incorrect because a tenancy at will is an estate in land terminable at the will of either the landlord or the tenant. No such relationship is intended under these facts.

4. **(D)** Reasonable restrictions on the use of the land—such as residential use only, prohibition of hunting on the premises, or painting the premises only a certain color-are generally upheld either as covenants at law or as equitable servitudes. Choices (A), (B), and (C) are reasonable types of restrictions. However, regarding restraints on alienation, the general rule is that ***any type of direct restraint upon alienation is null and void insofar as an estate in fee is concerned,*** based on strong public policy favoring free alienation. Burby, **Real Property,** p. 427. Therefore, choice (D) is the least likely restriction to be upheld since restricting the sale, mortgage, or other encumbrance of the land would amount to a direct restraint on alienation.

5. **(D)** This is an extremely tricky Multistate example dealing with conveyancing. Be aware that title established through adverse possession is free from encumbrance and of a character to assure quiet and peaceful enjoyment of the property by the vendee, but it is not a "marketable" title of record until there has been a judicial determination of such title. To show a record title by adverse possession requires a suit and the recording of a decree. Even though a court may determine that the vendor had title by adverse possession, the vendee did not bargain for that kind of title when the contract required a "marketable" title of record. Therefore, in accordance with the prevailing view, choice (D) is correct. This specific problem is referred to in Smith and Boyer, **Law of Property,** pg, 264.

6. **(B)** First of all, the conveyance created a life estate in Peter and Paula for their "joint lives" in Pineview. This life estate in the joint lives of Peter and Paula could only last until one of them died. In other words, at the death of either Peter or Paula, the life estate terminated. Secondly, Peter, Paula, and Patrick each have a contingent remainder in fee simple in Pineview. Contingent remainders are future interests created in favor of a transferee at the same time and in the same instrument as the

prior estate and they are subject to a condition precedent. The condition precedent is a happening or non-happening which must occur on or before the termination of the prior estate. In our factual situation, Peter, Paula, or Patrick's taking of the estate is subject to a condition precedent: that one of the parties must survive in order to take. Simply stated, the contingency of survival is expressed as the condition precedent.

7. **(A)** Here's a highly confusing Multistate Property example. Quite often, you may be confronted with a perplexing problem requiring mathematical computation. In this situation, don't get flustered! Stay cool! Obviously, this is an adverse possession problem. First, the facts indicate that the statutory period of adverse possession in this jurisdiction is 20 years. Looking back, the facts tell you that 12 years after Fisk took possession (of Grassacre), Luzinski died. Next, the facts indicate that nine years after his death, his son's guardian discovered Fisk in (adverse) possession of Grassacre. Now, adding the 12 years (before Luzinski's death) + the nine years (following his death) = 21 years. Thus, since Fisk's adverse possession is beyond the statutory period, choice (A) is correct. This is an *extremely popular* Multistate example because the *test maker* knows that many students will incorrectly choose either choice (C) or (D) because they are familiar with the rule wherein *one who is under a disability at the time of the accrual of the cause of action against the adverse possessor is given by statute time beyond the removal of his disability in which to bring his action.* This defense, however, is not applicable here because the *facts do not indicate that this Jurisdiction has enacted such a statute.*

8. **(C)** If one joint tenant conveys his interest in the property to another, even if the conveyance is done secretly, severance occurs, whereby the right of survivorship is severed and a tenancy in common results. Based on the facts presented, Louis would take an undivided one-half interest in Blackacre without right of survivorship.

9. **(A)** A tenancy by the entirety, unlike a joint tenancy, does not allow either party to convey away her interest in the property without the other's consent. As a result, Louis would not have any interest in Blackacre.

10. **(C)** One who by excavation or otherwise withdraws lateral support from her neighbor's land is **liable for the injury done to such land in its natural condition, regardless of negligence.** The common law right to lateral support is a right to the support of land in substantially its natural condition. It does not include the right to have the additional weight of artificial structures supported by the neighboring land. However, a defendant may be held liable for damage caused to structures if there **is proof of negligence** on his part. In the present example, X's land was essentially in its natural condition. As a result, choice (C) states the correct rule.

11. **(C)** A popular *Multistate* testing area deals with **surface waters.** Surface waters are those which come from rain, springs, and melting snow and ice, and simply follow the contours of the land and have not yet reached a natural water course or basin with well defined bed and banks. Under the common law rule (still followed in a majority of jurisdictions), sometimes called the "common enemy rule" because surface water is considered a common enemy, the lower tract is not burdened with any servitude in favor of the higher land and the owner of the lower tract has the

right to protect his lower tract from "the common enemy" or the flow of surface water by making any improvements which are suitable for the purpose.

12. **(A)** The possessor of real property has the right to the exclusive possession of the surface of the ground, the airspace above, and the soil underneath, the extent of which is determined by his exterior boundaries extended vertically upward and downward. This is commonly referred to as the "ad coelum" doctrine as to the upper space and was expressed in the Latin maxim, "cujus est solum ejus est usque ad coelum." Translated literally, "whose is the soil, his is to the sky or high heavens." In applying this rule, choice (A) is correct because *any use of the space above one's land which is unreasonable, improper, or interferes with the use and enjoyment of the surface can constitute a trespass.*

13. **(B)** One of the most popular Multistate testing areas deals with mortgages. The reason why mortgage problems are frequently tested on the exam is because the "general" bar review courses provide only a cursory review of this extremely important subject area. In this particular question, it has long been recognized *in equity that a deed absolute intended for security will in fact be construed as a mortgage.* This is not really surprising when it is remembered that the traditional form of the mortgage was a conveyance subject to defeasance, and that the equity of redemption was created by the equity court to protect the mortgagor after default. In order to preserve this equity of redemption various rules were formulated to prevent mortgages from limiting or clogging the equity of redemption. The most common example of such rules is the principle "once a mortgage always a mortgage." This, in effect, means that *a mortgagee cannot circumscribe the mortgagor's right to redeem by disguising the transaction as an outright conveyance.* In this example, the facts indicate that Quirk executed the deed absolute to Lama as additional security. Therefore, the deed will not extinguish Quirk's right of redemption since it (the deed absolute) will be construed as a mortgage and not an outright conveyance.

14. **(A)** *When the "mortgagee" under a deed absolute mortgage transfers to a bona fide purchaser, the mortgagor has no rights against the bona fide purchaser, but he does have an action for redemption against the "mortgagee "for the value of the land, or, at his election, the proceeds of the sale.* The theory is that the mortgagee now has the value of the land in his hands as a separate fund, and such fund as a substitute for the land may be redeemed by the mortgagor. Applying this rule to our given set of facts, Quirk has no right against Gonzales, the bona fide purchaser, but he does have an action for redemption against Lama, the mortgagee.

15. **(C)** Apparently, Toyota would have an implied easement in the walkway. An implied easement is created and proved not by the words of the conveyance but by all the circumstances surrounding the execution of the conveyance. It is based on the intention of the parties as inferred from the surrounding circumstances. There are five distinct requirements for the existence of an implied easement, all of which are present in the facts of this example. First, there must be two properties owned by one person who uses one of the pieces of property to serve the other piece of land. Second, there must be a conveyance of one part of the property to another person, the other part being retained by the conveyor. Third, the *quasi*-easement must be apparent at the time of the conveyance. Fourth, the *quasi*-easement must

be continuous, which means that the use of the *quasi*-servient tenement must be permanently adapted to serve the needs of the *quasi*-dominant tenement. Fifth, the *quasi*-easement must be (a) "reasonably necessary" to the convenient enjoyment of the *quasi*-dominant land if that tract is the property conveyed to the grantee, and (b) "strictly necessary" to the enjoyment of the *quasi*-dominant tenement if that tract is retained by the grantor. By virtue of the implied easement, Toyota has the right to enter the walkway for the purpose of repairing, maintaining, and improving the means by which the easement is enjoyed.

16. **(B)** John would succeed because **Shelley's Rule** operates as follows: if a life estate is conveyed to A and in the same instrument a remainder is given to A's heirs, then A will take a remainder in fee simple. In other words, ***A's life estate merges with the remainder to his heirs, thus giving A a fee simple absolute.***

17. **(A)** Choice (A) is correct because since the Rule is abolished, John would only acquire a life estate. As a result, in order to convey marketable title John's heirs must join in the conveyance of Blackacre. The remainder to John's heirs is treated as a vested remainder which does not merge with John's life estate.

18. **(C)** Choice (C) is correct because the old common law Doctrine of Worthier Title is construed today as a rule of construction whereby the grantor presumes not to create a remainder in his heirs, but rather intends to retain a reversion in himself. Refer to Justice Cardozo's opinion in the leading case of *Doctor v. Hughes,* 22 N.E. 211,1919.

19. **(C)** Smith and Boyer note that ***no conveyance is valid unless the description of the land sought to be conveyed is sufficient to identify the land.*** In this example, the facts indicate that Scenic-acre is a 40-acre tract of farmland. The leasehold agreement provided that Devine would have an option to purchase 10 acres of Scenicacre. Since the lease failed to identify or describe a *distinct piece* of Scenicacre, Faust's best argument is that the option should fail for lack of description. **Law of Property,** pg. 300.

20. **(D)** At common law, a tenant remains liable to pay rent even though because of fire, floods, storms, or other action of the elements or otherwise, the property is rendered totally uninhabitable unless the lease otherwise provides. So, therefore, if the decision is in favor of Mr. and Mrs. Tenner, it will most likely be because the doctrine of equitable conversion is inapplicable. Note that the equitable conversion doctrine applies only when there is an enforceable obligation to sell land. ***Caveat:*** Choice (C) is wrong because since this is an action at law (to recover money damages), the court will not apply equitable considerations (e.g., unjust enrichment) in resolving the dispute. Choice (B) is also wrong because a leasehold is considered an interest in land.

21. **(C)** Choice (C) is correct. Carr's interest in Blackacre would be a vested interest subject to complete divestiture. At the expiration of Burkhart's life estate, Carr would immediately be entitled to take possession of Blackacre. However, Carr's vested remainder (i.e., life estate in futuro in Blackacre) would be subject to complete divestiture upon the contingency of his redomiciling. Choice (A) is incorrect since a contingent remainder is a remainder limited so as to depend on an event or con-

dition which may not happen or be performed until after the termination of the preceding estate. Conversely, we are certain, here, that Burkhart's life estate will eventually terminate. Thus, although Carr may predecease Burkhart thereby terminating his actual enjoyment, his right to such enjoyment (i.e., vested remainder in Blackacre) is not uncertain. Choice (B) is incorrect since a "shifting" executory interest is a contingent remainder whereby one party's expectant interest is transferred or "shifted" to another upon the happening or non-happening of a particular contingency.

22. **(D)** Alternative (D) is correct since Drew's interest would be a shifting executory interest *pur autre vie*. An executory interest is an interest that divests the interest of another transferee (shifting executory interest) or that "follows a gap" or divests the interest of the transferor (springing executory interest). Furthermore, his shifting executory interest would be *pur autre vie,* since it would be an estate for the life of another (Carr).

23. **(D)** This is exactly the same situation that Smith and Boyer discuss in their hornbook on pg. 255. An executory contract for the sale of land requiring the seller to execute a deed conveying legal title upon payment of the full purchase price works an equitable conversion so as to make the purchaser the equitable owner of the land and the seller the equitable owner of the purchase price. The result is that the purchaser, the equitable owner of the land, takes the benefit of all subsequent increases in value and, at the same time, *becomes subject to all losses* not occasioned by the fault of the seller. Thus, the purchaser, to protect himself, either must procure his own insurance, or by appropriate provision in the contract, cast the risk upon the seller. He is not, however, entitled to recover insurance payments payable to the vendor. Note that choice (D) is a better answer than (A) because the equitable conversion doctrine which places the risk on the buyer requires such a result.

24. **(B)** Under the ***doctrine of equitable conversion*** the risk of loss from casualty and other fortuitous events is normally placed on the purchaser in the absence of controlling provisions in the contract. ***Equity thus considers the vendee as the owner of the land and the vendor as the owner of the purchase money.*** Smith and Boyer point out, however, that this rule is limited in its application to cases where the intention of the parties will not produce an inequitable result. For example, assume that A contracts to sell to B a certain piece of land which was to be used for the purpose of erecting a hotel. However, between the time the contract of sale was made and the time for delivery of the deed, the city council rezones the lot so that it could only be used for residential purposes. A now brings suit for specific performance. In this situation, Smith and Boyer note that the granting of specific performance would be unduly harsh and oppressive to B. Since the intent of the parties was defeated by the supervening event, specific performance should be denied. However, the denial of specific performance does not end the matter, but, instead, the vendor may proceed against the purchaser in a suit at law. **Real Property,** pg. 255. By analogy, if the court rules in favor of Beeson, it will be to avoid unjust enrichment.

25. **(C)** The "key" to this question is carefully interpreting the wording of the recording statute. According to the statutory language, the Runnymede recording act protects subsequent bona fide purchasers for value and without notice. As such, this

is an example of a pure "notice" type recording statute which generally provides that an unrecorded conveyance or other instrument is invalid as against a subsequent bona fide purchaser for value and without notice. Under this type of recording statute, *the subsequent **bona fide purchaser prevails over the prior interest whether the subsequent purchaser records or not.*** As a consequence, Fong will prevail over Eto because Fong was a subsequent bona fide purchaser without notice of Eto's deed.

26. **(C)** In order to be a *bona fide* purchaser protected under the recording act, one must (a) be subsequent, (b) pay value, (c) be without notice (the value must have actually been paid before notice), and (d) be of good faith. Be aware that ***recording statutes do not protect a subsequent claimant who has not paid more than a nominal consideration because he is not a purchaser.*** Therefore, in our case C and D (A's children) are not protected by the recording statute because they are not purchasers (as A purportedly *conveyed the property to them as a gift*).

27. **(B)** The ***doctrine of estoppel by deed*** (sometimes referred to as the "after-acquired title" doctrine) applies when a person executes a deed purporting to convey an estate in land which he does not have or which is larger than he has, and such person at a later date acquires such estate in such land; then the subsequently acquired estate will, by estoppel, pass to the grantee. In this example, once Fawn purchased the five-acre tract from Oswald, title inured to the benefit of Scott as evidenced by Oswald's quitclaim deed to Scott. Most importantly, Fawn held a mortgage on Greenacre. The mortgage instrument described the property interest as covering all 100-acres of Greenacre. Thus, when Scott defaulted and Fawn foreclosed, she purchased back the entire tract of Greenacre (including the five-acres previously owned by Oswald). Note that choice (A) is wrong because even though Fawn did not have good and marketable title to Greenacre initially, this title defect was subsequently cured by operation of the Fawn-Oswald transaction. Choice (C) is incorrect because at the moment Fawn acquired title to the five-acres from Oswald, title automatically inured to the benefit of Scott by virtue of the estoppel by deed doctrine. It is really irrelevant whether Oswald quitclaimed the property to Scott. This is tricky because in most states estoppel by deed will not be applied where the conveyance is by a quitclaim deed. In this question, however, remember that the Fawn-Scott conveyance was by warranty deed. That's why "after-acquired title" applies. In other words, even if Oswald didn't quitclaim the five-acre parcel to Scott, title would nonetheless inure to Scott's benefit.

28. **(C)** Here, Jeffrey and Beth acquired title to Blackacre as tenants in common (by descent). In a tenancy in common each tenant owns an undivided fractional part of the property; none owns the whole, as in joint tenancy. Note that choice (B) is wrong because Jeffrey's possession of Blackacre was not hostile and adverse since he in fact was the owner of the property (as a tenant in common).

29. **(A)** Tenant is still liable to Landlord for the $500 monthly rental despite the fact that he can no longer reside in the building. At common law, the general rule is that a tenant remains liable to pay rent even though because of fire, floods, or other unforeseen action, the property is rendered totally uninhabitable. Please note that it is possible for the parties to provide in a lease for certain excuses for nonpayment of rental. But in our hypothetical, no such provision was made in the lease.

30. **(B)** The general rule provides that a tenant who covenants to keep the leasehold premises in good repair is liable under such a covenant for all defects (except normal wear and tear) regardless of their cause. As a result, a tenant remains liable for any defects caused by himself, third persons, and even acts of God. Choices (A), (C), and (D) are all incorrect statements of law.

31. **(B)** A covenant in a lease to pay (fire) insurance is held to "run with the land." In this regard, note that a covenant to pay insurance is capable of running *if and only if* the landlord is bound to use the proceeds for repair or replacement. It is important to understand that Tony's assignment of his leasehold interest to Rick did not relieve or extinguish Tony's contractual obligations under his lease with Harry. In short, an assignment does not release the tenant from his contract obligations to the landlord under the terms of this original leasehold agreement. To be sure, a lease is a contract as well as a conveyance.

32. **(B)** The most accurate statement regarding a covenant (in the lease) which requires the tenant to keep the premises in repair is that he is liable under such a covenant for all defects (except normal wear and tear) regardless of their cause. As a result, a tenant is liable for any defects caused by himself, third persons, and even acts of God.

33. **(A)** In reiteration, where a tenant-assignor transfers all of his leasehold interest to an assignee, such assignment *does not release* the tenant from his contract obligations to the landlord under the terms of the lease. This is true even when the assignee, thereafter, assigns/transfers his leasehold interest to a sub-assignee.

34. **(C)** In accordance with the **Rule in Dumpor's Case,** if a landlord grants consent to one transfer (e.g., Tony's assignment to Rick), he waives his right to avoid future transfers, assigns, or sub-leases in violation of a prohibition in the lease against such transfers. By the same token, if the lessee/assignee pays rent to the landlord and such rent is accepted by him, in spite of the fact that the transfer was in violation of the lease, the landlord will be deemed to have waived his right to avoid the transfer.

35. **(C)** After purchasing the property at the sheriff's sale, Thomas, as record title owner, would no longer remain obligated under the leasehold contract. As such, choice (C) is correct because the sheriff's sale would vitiate Thomas' obligation to make any further rental payments to Leonard.

36. **(D)** Thomas is liable for the damage to the floors caused by his failure to replace the shingles since a tenant for years is legally bound to make such ordinary repairs on the leased property as will avoid serious injury to the property. Thus, Thomas' failure to make the necessary repairs would make him liable for such permissive waste.

37. **(D)** Leonard may not recover for rent due from sublessee since there is no privity of estate between landlord and sublessee. Leonard's only cause of action remains against the tenant under their original leasehold agreement.

38. **(A)** The power of eminent domain may be delegated directly or indirectly to a private person or enterprise subject to the requirements that the taking be (a) for a public use and (b) just compensation be given.

39. **(D)** In answering "tier" questions of this type, you should read each statement (i.e., I, II, III, and IV) and determine whether it is *true* or *false*. Be advised that statement II is false because this question deals with adverse possession, not licenses. As a consequence, choices (A) and (C) can be eliminated. In choosing between alternatives (B) and (D), the latter is preferred because it establishes the necessary state of mind required for adverse possession. Possession of real property requires acts of *dominion* and *control* with an intent to possess and exclude others.

40. **(A)** By virtue of the assignment, *the assignee (i.e., Moore) falls into privity of estate with the landlord and he is liable on all covenants in the original lease which "run with the land."* Since the covenant to pay taxes, under the original leasehold agreement between landlord-Donaldson and tenant-McGuirk, "runs with the land," Moore, as assignee, would be held liable. In light of the fact that Moore, as assignee, is liable on the covenant to pay taxes, all other choices are incorrect.

41. **(A)** Under the terms of their original leasehold agreement, McGuirk would remain liable for the rent in arrears. McGuirk's assignment to Moore would not operate as an extinguishment of his duty to pay rent to Donaldson under the terms of their original agreement. An assignment does not release the tenant from his contractual obligation to the landlord under the lease. To be sure a lease is a contract as well as a conveyance. Choice (B) is erroneous because Donaldson's notice (of the assignment) is irrelevant to the effectuation of Moore's obligations under the assignment. Choices (C) and (D) are erroneous for the above reasons.

42. **(D)** Since the sublessee Burger is not in privity of estate with the landlord, the sublessee is not subject to the covenants or terms of the leasehold agreement. Therefore, Moore will remain liable for the entire $300 rental. As a result, choices (A) and (B) are incorrect. Choice (C) is wrong because McGuirk, as assignor, would not be the *only* party liable.

43. **(B)** The question of law presented here is, namely, when there is a partial taking of a leasehold estate by condemnation and the remaining portion is susceptible for occupation, shall the contractual monthly rental be abated pro tanto for the part taken during the remainder of the time of the lease? The majority rule is that rentals are not abated in this situation, but rather the tenant is obligated to continue the payment of the rentals provided in the lease contract and must look to an apportionment of the damages assessed against the condemning authority based on the reduced value of his lease.

44. **(A)** Choice (A) is the most accurate statement. The question asks in so many words "What is the legal effect of the non-assignability clause in the Landley-Tennance contract?" The non-assignability provision had no legal effect. Since Tennance's transfer (of the premises) to Aruba constituted a sublease, not an assignment, the said provision would have no legal effect. Choice (C) is less correct because, although factually true, it does *not* answer the question asked. You must know the distinction between an assignment and a sublease. An assignment is a transfer of a tenant's *entire* leasehold estate to another; whereas a sublease is a transfer of anything less than a tenant's entire leasehold estate. In the example here, Tennance entered into his leasehold agreement with Aruba *one year after* his contract with Landley.

45. **(A)** In the case of a sublease, privity of estate and privity of contract exist between the original landlord and tenant. Similarly, privity of estate and privity of contract exist between the tenant and subtenant. However, neither privity of contract nor privity of estate exists between the original landlord and subtenant. Therefore, the landlord cannot sue the subtenant. As a consequence, Landley may not recover against subtenants Aruba and Simon. He may only recover against tenant Tennance under the terms of their original leasehold contract.

46. **(D)** As noted in the previous explanation, there is privity of estate and privity of contract between the landlord and the tenant. Likewise, privity of estate and privity of contract exist between the tenant and subtenant. However, neither privity of contract nor privity of estate exists between the landlord and the subtenant.

47. **(B)** At common law, a landlord generally does not impliedly warrant that the leased premises are suitable for any particular purpose, and he is not liable for a dangerous condition existing on the leased premises. Normally, the doctrine of *caveat emptor* prevails, but there are two notable exceptions. First, Smith and Boyer point out that "A landlord may be liable in tort to the tenant, his guests, licensees, and invitees, if at the ***commencement of the lease there is a dangerous condition which the landlord knows or should know about*** and the discovery of which would not likely occur by the tenant exercising due care." **Property,** pg. 138. Based on this exception, choice (B) is correct because the dangerous condition existed at the commencement of the leasehold period (note: the facts indicate that Brown was injured on the *first day* Yale took possession of the warehouse). The second exception is that a landlord in the lease of a completely furnished dwelling for a short period of time impliedly warrants the fitness of the premises and the furnishings.

48. **(B)** In 1960 the state of Sylvania's interest in Pocono Woods would be described as a fee simple subject to condition subsequent, which means fee simple subject to being terminated by exercise of the power of termination or right of re-entry for condition broken. The important characteristic which distinguishes this type of estate from a fee simple determinable is that the estate will continue in the grantee, or his successors, unless and until the power of termination is exercised. Although no particular words are essential to create an estate on condition subsequent, the use in the conveyance of the traditional words of condition – "upon condition that," "provided that," or "but if" – coupled with a provision for re-entry by the transferor or the occurrence of the stated event will normally be construed to manifest an intention to create an estate on condition subsequent.

49. **(D)** A profit-a-pendre is similar to an easement, in that it is a non-possessory interest. The holder of the profit is entitled to enter upon the servient tenement and take the substance of the land (e.g., minerals, trees, oil, or game) subject to the privilege. In this regard, a profit, like an easement, may be appurtenant or in gross.

50. **(C)** Woody will not succeed since the Director's objective in the clearing of the timber was for the purpose of developing a recreational area. Although Crockett was not privileged (under the terms of Woody's deed over to Sylvania) to use the tract for his own commercial advantage, the court will look to the ultimate purpose for which the land was to be used (i.e., recreational park). Thus, the court will conclude

that Woody's original intention and expectation in conveying Pocono Woods to the state was not materially or adversely affected.

51. **(C)** O would win since A's possession was not continuous. For one to hold property adversely, his possession must be (1) actual and exclusive, (2) open and notorious, (3) continuous and peaceable (meaning without any interruption), and (4) hostile and adverse. In this case, since A's possession was interrupted he didn't fulfill the statutory requirement of continuous possession for 20 years.

52. **(D)** Choice (D) is correct since the period of adverse possession of one possessor can be tacked to the period of adverse possession of another possessor when there is privity (e.g. blood or contract) between the two.

53. **(A)** Since A was in continuous possession of Greenacre from 1957 to 1977, he would acquire title by adverse possession. As a result, choice (A) is correct. Note that choice (B) is incorrect because the facts do not disclose that B was a remainderman or had a remainder interest in Greenacre. Rather, O simply devised the property to B in 1961. As a consequence, B did not have a remainder interest but a present possessory interest as of 1961.

54. **(C)** According to Smith and Boyer, a joint tenant has no right of contribution against the other joint tenants for repairs or improvements he has made, but if partition is had the court in making an equitable division of the proceeds will take into consideration the expenditures made by one tenant for repairs and improvements. **Law of Property,** pg. 66. Be advised that *partition proceedings are under the jurisdiction of a court of equity.* So therefore, applying the maxim "that one who seeks equity must do equity, the court is free to adjust accounts between the parties in a fair and equitable manner." Be advised that choice (C) is correct because "one concurrent owner may be charged for use and occupation of the property (reasonable rental value) and he may be given credit for the value of improvements erected, repairs made, and taxes paid." Burby, **Real Property,** pg. 233.

55. **(B)** Under the unity of possession, each co-tenant is entitled to possess and enjoy the whole of the property subject to the equal right of his co-tenant. *If one tenant wrongfully excludes another co-tenant from possession of the whole or any part of the whole of the property, such conduct amounts to an ouster.* Here, choice (B) is correct because there is no evidence that Hunter was wrongfully excluding Trent from Blackacre. Note that choice (A) is wrong because Burby points out that "possession may become adverse if the co-tenants are excluded from possession (i.e., ouster) or if the co-tenants are specifically notified of the adverse claim or can be charged with notice because of the acts of the possessor." **Real Property,** pg. 232.

56. **(B)** Birch's proper cause of action should be based on nuisance, rather than trespass. The basic distinction which is now recognized is that trespass is an invasion of the plaintiff's interest in the exclusive possession of his land, whereas nuisance is an interference with his use and enjoyment of it. In all likelihood, Ash has an implied easement for his sewer pipe from parcel "A" across parcels "B" and "C." It is generally agreed that in cases involving an implied reservation (or *quasi-easement*) in favor of the grantor, there must be *reasonable necessity* for the existence of the implied easement.

57. **(B)** An easement may arise by implication if the existence of the easement is strictly (or reasonably) necessary for the beneficial use of the land. The creation of such an easement is based upon the presumed intent of the grantor and grantee. If the claim is made that the easement arose out of a prior conveyance, there must be proof of the fact that at one time both the dominant and servient estates were under one ownership. Technically, alternative (A) is correct, but choice (B) is the preferred answer because the present example is an illustration of an *implied* easement appurtenant. With respect to choice (C), an easement (or profit) may also be acquired by prescription in a manner similar to that by which ownership of a possessory estate may be acquired by adverse possession.

58. **(D)** The right to subjacent support means support from underneath the surface of the land as distinguished from the sides, but the rights involved are substantially the same as those involved in lateral support. Thus, the right to lateral (and subjacent) support does not include the right to have the additional weight of artificial structures on the land held up by the neighboring land. However, if there is negligence on the part of the wrongdoer who removes lateral or subjacent support, then the wrongdoer is liable for all damages which naturally and proximately result. In this hypothesis, since Catskill's land was in an improved state with a dwelling erected on the land, he must show that Ash acted negligently.

59. **(C)** If there are artificial structures on the land and the land in its natural condition would be injured by the taking away of lateral support, then there are two distinct views as to the damages recoverable: (a) in some states the recovery will include both the damages to the land **and** the damage to the artificial structures thereon (called the English rule, (b) **but in the majority of states the recovery is limited to damage to the land in its natural condition and may not include any damage to the artificial structures on the land (called the American rule).** The theory of the American rule is that to permit the wronged landowner to recover for damage to his buildings is in substance a requirement that the adjoining landowner's land furnish lateral support for both the land and the buildings of the plaintiff.

60. **(A)** Every leasehold includes the following elements: (a) an estate in the tenant, (b) a reversion in the landlord, (c) **exclusive possession and control of the land in the tenant,** and (d) generally, a contract between the parties. The first three elements constitute privity of estate, and the fourth is privity of contract. Whereas in a **lease** exclusive possession must reside in the tenant, in a **license** the possession remains in the licensor and the licensee has a mere privilege of being on the land without being treated as a trespasser. Smith and Boyer, **Real Property,** p. 48. Ordinarily a lodging contract does not create a landlord-tenant relationship but only that of licensor and licensee, whereby the occupant contracts for the use of a room and facilities without a possessory interest in the land. Exclusive possession and control remains in the landowner. In this question Bobby Saul, as a hotel guest, does not have exclusive possession and control of his hotel room. He is a licensee rather than a tenant. Furthermore, the facts do not strongly support a periodic tenancy since his oral agreement with the Four Seasons Hotel was not referred to as a "lease," nor was the weekly payment referred to as "rent." Therefore, no seven-day prior notice will be required. Thus, in the absence of any leasehold Bobby will owe no additional balance beyond the day he checks out. Choice (A) is correct.

61. **(B)** The swampland is not now and cannot be made usable for the growing of crops. It seems to be capable of growing trees only. This swampland, as far as the facts disclose, has never been used and at the time of the taking effect of Tim's life estate was not being used for the production of lumber. Tim is the first to cut timber thereon. At this point an analogy may assist in the analysis and understanding of the problem. It is well settled that a tenant for life or for years has a right to continue the operation of old mines on the leased premises for the reason that such is the use to which the land has been put or is being put at the time of the beginning of the tenant's estate. The lease implies that such use may be continued. On the other hand, such tenants have no right to open new mines and appropriate the minerals therefrom. The reason is clear. It has taken eons of time to produce the minerals which underlay the land. It is the very substance of which the land is made and that corpus should not be available for consumption or destruction by a tenant of a limited interest in the premises, unless of course the lease is made for the very purpose of mining. Likewise, it has taken generations of time to produce the hardwood forests of the swampland and the value of that forest is the very heart and substance of that portion of Blue Bayou. It should not be available for consumption and destruction by a tenant of a limited estate as against the reversioner or remainderman who owns the inheritance. Therefore, Tim should be permanently enjoined from cutting any more trees on the swampland, and should account for the proceeds from the sale of the timber which was cut on the swampland.

62. **(B)** *Ameliorating waste is a change in the physical characteristics of the occupied premises by an unauthorized act of the tenant which increases the value of the property.* Herein, any change in the characteristics of land which makes it more productive and adds to the store of consumable goods should be given all the protection which sound legal principles permit. It takes much time, labor, and power to convert timberland into tillable fields for the production of annual crops. The law takes account of such by awarding to him the timber which is removed for such purpose. Thus, the tenant for life or for years has a right to use land as good husbandry dictates. As such, this usually includes the right to transform timberland into arable land for the plow, provided of course the soil can be made suitable for such purpose.

63. **(C)** It is of utmost importance to understand and recognize the difference between actions at law and in equity. *Injunctive relief is an equitable remedy.* Thus, choice (C) is correct because equitable waste is an injury to the reversionary interest in land which is inconsistent with good husbandry and is recognized only by the equity courts. Be aware that it (i.e., equitable waste) does not constitute *legal* waste as recognized by the courts of law. On the other hand, all other alternatives are incorrect because (a) voluntary waste, (b) permissive waste, and (c) ameliorating waste are types of *legal* waste, wherein the life tenant or tenant for years will be liable for monetary damages.

64. **(B)** Haynes would be liable for removal of the hog house but not the corn crib. For an article of personal property to become a fixture on land, it is necessary that (1) there be an annexation of the article to the land either actually or constructively, (2) the article be adapted to the use for which the land is used, and (3) there be an intention on the part of the annexer that the article become a fixture. With respect to the hog house, the facts clearly state that it was built of brick and mortar

and affixed to a cement foundation which extended twenty-four inches into the soil. Thus, the fact that the hog house was actually built into the soil and cannot be removed without lifting the cement foundation out of its resting place (and causing complete destruction of the hog house as a building) clearly indicates an intention to make it a fixture. Conversely, the fact that the corn crib can be removed from the property with practically no injury to the freehold would indicate that there would be little economic waste in its removal. Therefore, it seems proper to permit Haynes to remove the corn crib without being liable for waste.

65. **(B)** When land has been mortgaged and thereafter a chattel is attached to the land and becomes a fixture, the claim of the mortgagee takes priority over the claim of the mortgagor. Moreover, if a tenant of the mortgagor adds a chattel, as a fixture of the realty, it inures to the benefit of the mortgagee of the real property. As a result, Farm Life Insurance Co. would prevail over Abigail (the mortgagor), since the removal of the hog house would constitute waste. It is important to note that trade fixtures are chattels which are annexed to the land by a tenant for the purpose and convenience of his trade or business on the land. Usually this doctrine is applied to factory machinery, store and shop equipment, or temporary partitions in industrial establishments. However, difficulty exists when this doctrine is applied to buildings or to additional extensions to the buildings already present on the land.

66. **(C)** After Smith's death in 1930, Dixie's interest in Winterthur could best be described as a shifting executory interest (or executory devise as it was created by will), which divests the preceding estate upon the happening or non-happening of a stated event. Executory devises are interests which are identical with springing and shifting uses, except that they are created by will, instead of by deed. Thus, in 1930 Smith devised a fee simple to his son, Smitty, and his heirs, which was subject to Dixie's executory interest. If the event happens (Smitty dies without issue) then Dixie will have a possessory estate in fee.

67. **(C)** In a suit to quiet title to Winterthur, Dixie would prevail. At the time of Smitty's death on January 1, 1976, (without issue) Dixie's executory interest was executed into a legal estate in fee. In fact, Dixie's interest vested automatically upon Smitty's death without issue, without any affirmative act on her part.

68. **(C)** Equitable conversion applies when there is an enforceable obligation to sell land. The doctrine treats interests in land as if the land had already been converted into personal property. The doctrine states that when the sales contract is made, equity then considers the vendee as the owner of the land and the vendor as the owner of the purchase money. Applying the facts of the case to this doctrine, Stevens would be construed as the equitable owner of the land on January 20, 1979, when the barn was destroyed by fire. As a result, Stevens as equitable owner would become subject to all losses not occasioned by the fault of the seller. Therefore, if the court determined that Stevens held equitable title to Winterthur on January 20th, he would be unsuccessful in his lawsuit against Barnes.

69. **(A)** At common law, since a tenant was deemed to receive an estate in land, his rights and duties were treated as **independent** of the landlord's rights and duties. Thus, if the landlord promised to keep the property in repair, a breach of this promise **did not relieve the tenant from the duty of paying rent.** According to the common

law rationale, the rent was owed as payment for the estate, and the promise to do repairs was merely a collateral promise which could be enforced only by a separate contractual suit brought by the tenant. This doctrine is generally referred to as the *independence of covenants.* As a result, choices (C) and (D) are incorrect. Choice (B) is wrong because the landlord will prevail because the premises were not *un*inhabitable (the basis for constructive eviction), rather than because the tenant failed to perform the re-painting himself. In other words, self-help is not an appropriate remedy inasmuch as the tenant had no duty to make such repairs.

70. **(C)** The Statute of Frauds requires a writing *(1) identifying the parties, (2) describing the subject matter, (3) stating the purchase price, and (4) signed by the party to be charged.* The writing Gamma delivered to Delta did not state any consideration — it was intended as a gift. Furthermore, it was not an effective gift because it was only a *promise to convey.* An effective gift requires a *present transfer* of an interest. *If the transfer is to take effect in futuro, it is a mere promise to make a gift and unenforceable for lack of consideration.* Smith and Boyer, **Survey of the Law of Property**, p. 469. Therefore, choice (A) is incorrect, and choice (C) is the correct answer. Since Gamma's writing did not create an assignment, choice (B) is incorrect. Choice (D) is incorrect. Delta does not have an adequate remedy at law for lack of consideration, nor will specific performance be granted for lack of mutuality.

71. **(B)** A mortgagee has *both an in personam* claim against the mortgagor on the debt or obligation *and an in rem action* against the security. As a result, choice (B) is correct because mortgagee-Epsilon has an in personam action against mortgagor-Gamma. Note that choices (A) and (C) are wrong because Gamma's conveyance to Delta was by a quitclaim deed. A quitclaim deed usually contains *no* assurances; it simply operates as a transfer to the grantee of whatever interest, if any, the grantor happens to own.

72. **(C)** In this case, Epsilon, the mortgagee, is bringing a claim against Delta, the grantee. Since the facts state that the deed "made no reference to the mortgage," it is presumed that Delta took "subject to" Gamma's mortgage. Therefore, Delta will not be personally liable because she did not promise to pay the mortgage debt. Choice (C) is correct. *Note:* Only Gamma as mortgagor would be liable to Epsilon under these facts.

73. **(C)** The termination date of Jay's lease was January 31, 1980. The facts state that on February 1, 1979, Jay had made the yearly rental payment of $3500 to Hancock for the year 1979. Therefore, Jay had complied with his obligation in accordance with the original leasehold agreement. It is important to note that Hancock and Jay entered into an oral leasehold agreement for five years. In the majority of states, such a parol lease for a period not to exceed one year from the making thereof is valid. However, parol leases which exceed the one year's time period are generally *invalid* to create such a tenancy for years because of the Statute of Frauds. But as a general rule, the Statute of Frauds *only* affects the duration of the lease. Thus any covenants and conditions agreed upon in the lease, such as the rental obligations, are still valid as long as the landlord-tenant relationship exists.

74. **(C)** The grantor and grantee indices are utilized in most jurisdictions today in the title search of real estate records. In the grantor index, all conveyances are indexed

alphabetically and chronologically under the initial letter of the grantor's surname. In the grantee index, a like index is made of conveyances under the initial letter of the grantee's surname. A title searcher must trace both indices in order to complete his search. Therefore, Miss Kitty should properly trace Fred's name in both the grantor index and the grantee index.

75. **(D)** In Slotnick's action to enjoin Eagleson's use of Looney Lane, Eagleson will lose because he has no legal right to drive over Looney Lane. Choice (D) is correct. Looney constructed Looney Lane as a private road for use only by owners of the lots in the subdivision. The road was not intended to benefit outside landowners, such as Eagleson, who did not reside in the subdivision. Choice (B) is incorrect because an implied easement is based on the *inferred intention of the parties, namely the grantor and the grantee.* Use of Looney Lane arises between Looney, the grantor, and her grantees, such as Slotnick. Eagleson, on the other hand, was Dooley's grantee, and constructed the access road to Looney Lane after he purchased Parcel 2 from Dooley. Choice (A) is incorrect because an easement by necessity requires, inter alia, that at the time of the conveyance one part of the land is being used for the benefit of the other part (a quasi-easement). Smith and Boyer, **Survey of the Law of Property,** p. 384. Looney Lane was not used by Eagleson until after he built the access road connecting Parcel 2 with it. Choice (C) is incorrect under the facts stated since Eagleson could use the access road he constructed to reach Lincoln Boulevard.

76. **(C)** Perez will not be able to enjoin Eagleson's use of the driveway across Parcel 1 because Eagleson has an easement by necessity. Choice (C) is correct. An ***easement by necessity*** requires the following: (1) existence of a ***quasi-easement*** at the time of conveyance; (2) ***apparent use;*** (3) ***continuous use; and*** (4) ***reasonable necessity, where the grantee receives the dominant tenement.*** A quasi-easement existed when Dooley conveyed to Eagleson. At that time Parcel 2 had no other access to a public road, thereby allowing Dooley an easement by strict necessity over Perez's land, which passed to Eagleson upon conveyance of Parcel 2. Choice (D) is incorrect because Dooley's use was not adverse to anyone—he owned both parcels—until 1986, so no prescriptive easement is possible. Choices (A) and (B) reach the wrong conclusion and are incorrect because of the existence of the easement by necessity.

77. **(B)** Under the doctrine of ***riparian rights*** there are two theories, the ***"natural flow"*** theory and the ***"reasonable use"*** theory. The former stresses the right of each owner to have the natural state of the stream or lake undiminished in both quality and quantity. The latter stresses maximum use by each owner provided it does not interfere with like use by other owners. Also, under the riparian doctrine, use of water for *natural* purposes—domestic use, watering of stock—is superior to use of water for *artificial* purposes—irrigation, mining, industry. Smith and Boyer, **Survey of the Law of Property**, pp. 186-189. Therefore, based on these rules, Carson will prevail over DuVall in accordance with answer choice (B). Choice (A) is incorrect because the theory of riparian rights allows a lower riparian (DuVall) to sue an upper riparian (Carson) where the latter's use materially affects the quantity or quality of water—the natural flow—or unreasonably causes damages—reasonable use. Choice (C) is incorrect because DuVall's use was only "adverse" since 1986, not for the statutory 15 years. Choice (D) is incorrect since it states the rule under the prior appropriation theory.

78. **(B)** In this example, Grant has a fee simple subject to a condition subsequent, which is an estate in fee simple that may be terminated by the conveyor, or those claiming under him upon the happening of a named event. Note that the important characteristic which distinguishes this type of estate from a fee simple determinable is that *the estate will continue in the grantee, or his successors, unless and until the power of termination is exercised.* The basic difference, therefore, is that the fee simple determinable automatically expires by force of the special limitation contained in the instrument creating the estate, when the stated contingency occurs, whereas the fee simple on condition subsequent continues despite the breach of the specified condition until it is divested or cut short by the exercise by the grantor of his power to terminate. Although no particular words are essential to create an estate on condition subsequent, the use in the conveyance of the traditional words of condition – "upon condition that," "provided that," "but if" – *coupled with a provision for re-entry* by the grantor will be construed to create an estate on condition subsequent.

79. **(B)** An equitable servitude may be extinguished by the existence of conditions which make the purpose and object of the servitude impossible to achieve, such as change in the character of the neighborhood from a residential to a business area. Note choice (D) is incorrect because a zoning ordinance will not generally invalidate an equitable servitude.

80. **(C)** This is an example of the extinguishment of an easement *by merger.* An easement appurtenant is terminated by merger if the dominant and servient tenements come into common ownership. Choice (A) is wrong because failure to use an easement or profit will not result in its extinguishment. Note, however, that non-use coupled with physical acts (clearly indicating the user's intent to abandon) may be sufficient to effectuate an extinguishment. As a general review, remember that easements (or profits) may be terminated in the following ways: (1) by merger, (2) written release, (3) non-use + other acts indicating an intent to abandon, (4) prescription, (5) destruction of servient tenement, (6) tax sale of servient tenement, or (7) estoppel.

81. **(A/D)** The owner of a possessory estate in land is under a duty to use his possessory rights in a reasonable manner. Physical damage to the land is waste if it causes a substantial diminution in the value of estates owned by others in the same land. Burby, **Real Property**, p. 33. However, the owner of an estate in fee simple has almost complete freedom of action with respect to the use and enjoyment of the land. Austin is a fee simple owner and as an incident of possession has "the right to the exclusive possession of the surface of the ground, the airspace above, and the soil underneath." Smith and Boyer, **Survey of the Law of Property**, p. 71. Choice (D) is correct. Choice (A) is also correct, since the right to remove oil is an incident of possession of *any* fee simple interest, whether a fee simple absolute or a fee simple defeasible. Removal of oil turns on Austin's right of exclusive possession. Furthermore, remember in this case that Rosalina, as the holder of the shifting executory interest, has no *vested* interest in Alpine Flats, but rather a *mere expectancy*, until such time that Molly might die without children. Until then, Austin can remove oil and his doing so as a fee simple owner does not constitute waste.

82. **(D)** Here's a rather confusing Multistate example where all four answer choices are technically incorrect. However, by process of elimination alternative (D) is the "best of the worst." Choices (A) and (B) are incorrect because once Molly died without issue, Rosalina's shifting executory interest "vested" and Austin's fee was cut off. Choice (C) is wrong because Austin's fee does not "revert" back to the grantor-Longhorn but shifts to the benefit of the grantee-Rosalina. Thus, choice (D) is the best answer even though Austin's fee terminated at Molly's death.

83. **(C)** An ***easement by prescription*** arises by adverse use of the servient tenement by the dominant tenant for the period of the statute of limitations. To mature such an easement against a landowner, the use must be (a) ***adverse*** as distinct from permissive; (b) in derogation of right rather than in subordination to the rights of the landowner; (c) ***open and notorious;*** (d) ***continuous*** and without interruption; and (e) ***for the period of prescription.*** See Smith and Boyer, **Law of** Property, p. 387. Since Stein openly and notoriously used the northeast portion of Hillacre to gain access to Grassacre for the 20-year period, as required by statute, he obtained an easement by prescription. This easement passed on to Grich, who was in privity with Stein by means of the 1980 sales contract. Therefore, Grich's rights are enforceable against the whole world and he will prevail against Erika. Choice (C) is the correct answer.

84. **(B)** Choice (B) is the preferred alternative since a subsequent bona fide purchaser without notice of a prior mortgage (e.g., the 1898 Warner-Miller mortgage) outside the chain of title would prevail over the prior mortgagee. It is important to note that Tidwell would not be charged with "constructive notice" of the 1898 Warner-Miller mortgage since Warner did not acquire title to the property until 1900. Therefore, Tidwell would be charged with constructive notice of the 1900 devise from Evers to Warner and the 1850 conveyance from the State of Baden to Evers. In sum, the 1898 Warner-Miller mortgage would fall outside Tidwell's chain of title.

85. **(D)** Under notice-type recording statutes, ***an unrecorded conveyance or other instrument is invalid*** as against a subsequent bona fide purchaser (creditor or mortgagee) for value and without notice. Under this type of statute the subsequent bona fide purchaser prevails over the prior interest whether the subsequent purchaser records or not. Insofar as the subsequent purchaser is concerned, there is no premium on his race to the recorder's office; his priority is determined upon his status at the time he acquires his deed or mortgage.

86. **(D)** There can be no rescission of an executory contract for the sale of land merely because of lack of title (e.g., existence of an encumbrance) in the vendor *prior to the date* when performance is due (on the "closing" date). Neither can a vendee place the vendor in default by tendering payment and demanding a deed in advance of the time and under circumstances not contemplated by the contract.

87. **(B)** Here, it is clear that Vincent's covenant against encumbrances was breached the very instant he conveyed Breezyacre to Baggett because the encumbrance of the 1898 mortgage burdened Breezyacre at that time. Note that, in this regard, even though the mortgagee never forecloses or threatens to foreclose and the subsequent purchaser is never called upon to pay off the encumbrance, there is, nevertheless, a breach of covenant and the covenantee may recover damages.

88. **(B)** According to Smith and Boyer, every easement appurtenant requires two pieces of land which are owned by two different persons. The two pieces of land involved are (1) *the dominant tenement,* which is the land whose owner is benefited by the easement, and (2) *the servient tenement,* which is the land whose owner is burdened by the easement. The owner of the dominant tenement is called the dominant tenant and the owner of the servient tenement is called the servient tenant. Second, when an easement appurtenant is created (either by conveyance or prescription) over a servient tenement, the boundaries and extent of such easement become fixed and are binding on both the servient and the dominant tenants. It is important to remember that neither tenant has the right to change the location of such easement or change the boundaries of the servient or dominant tenement(s). In this example, many students will incorrectly choose choice (A). Here, choice (B) is the best answer because Amos has an easement appurtenant between Blackacre (the dominant tenement) and Whiteacre (the servient tenement). He is attempting to use Whiteacre in connection with Greenacre, another tract of land that is not part of the dominant tenement. If, on the contrary, Amos attempted to make excessive use of Whiteacre in relationship to Blackacre, then choice (A) would be correct. For example, if Amos had a right of way for crossing Whiteacre (from Blackacre) on foot or by bicycle, then it would be beyond the scope of the easement for him to cross Whiteacre (from Blackacre) by automobile. This, however, is *not* the situation. Therefore, choice (B) is the correct answer.

89. **(C)** This is a *classic* Multistate Property example where a substantial number of students will incorrectly choose choice (D). The *test maker* knows that many students will be led astray by viewing this as a trespass-type question. In trespass, of course, the plaintiff is entitled to relief if he shows an intentional unprivileged entry. If he does so, the plaintiff is then entitled at least to nominal damages and possibly an injunction prohibiting further trespass. This example, however, does not really deal with the issue of trespass. Rather, what we have here is a **boundary line agreement** between Mays and Mantle. As a general rule, judicial recognition is extended to boundary line agreements even if not executed with the formalities prescribed by the Statute of Frauds. Burby notes that application of the doctrine usually requires proof that the parties were not informed as to the true boundary line, that there was an express or implied agreement as to its locations, and possession that conformed to the agreement. As such, Snider's (i.e., the grantee's) proper cause of action is not against Mays for trespass, but rather it is against Mantle (as grantor) for breach of covenant against encumbrances. An encumbrance that affects ownership but does not interfere with the use of land constitutes a breach of covenant against encumbrances. This is even true if the grantee knew of the encumbrance at the time he acquired ownership. **Real Property,** pg. 310.

90. **(C)** Before attempting to answer this question, first determine what interest, if any, Reed has in Greenacre. As we know, Bradley (the grantor) conveyed the property "to Martina for life with remainder to Reed, if he be living." Does Reed take a vested or contingent remainder under this conveyance? The answer is that Reed takes a vested remainder. *A vested remainder is one which is limited to an ascertained person who has the right to immediate possession if and when the prior estate is terminated.* It may be subject to no other condition, in which case it is said to be indefeasibly or absolutely vested. In that case it is certain to become an estate in possession. But it may (as in this example) be subject to a condition subsequent

(i.e., Reed's surviving Martina) which will divest the remainderman of his estate. But it is, nevertheless, vested until divested. On the other hand, *a contingent remainder is one which is subject to a condition precedent.* It is one which will not vest *until* the happening of an event or the ascertainment of a person. In our case, Reed has a vested remainder although it may be totally divested since it is subject to the condition subsequent that he be living at the termination of Martina's prior life estate. Note that *a tenant for life or for years is liable to the (vested) remainderman or reversioner for voluntary waste;* therefore Martina is liable to Reed for an accounting of the proceeds from the coal sales. In addition, *a vested remainderman has a right to compel the prior estate owner to pay taxes and interest on encumbrances to the extent of the value of rents and profits.* Consequently, choice (C) is correct.

Multistate Nuance Chart

FUTURE INTERESTS

VESTED REMAINDER	CONTINGENT REMAINDER
1. Is vested.	1. Is *not* vested.
2. Is *not* subject to the Rule Against Perpetuities.	2. Is subject to the Rule Against Perpetuities
3. Is limited to an ascertained person who has the right to immediate possession if and when the prior estate is terminated.	3. Is subject to a condition precedent; it will not vest until the happening of an event or the ascertainment of a person.
4. Remainderman has right against prior estate owner (e.g., life tenant) for waste.	4. Remainderman has *no* right against prior estate owner (e.g., life tenant) for waste.
5. Remainderman has right to compel prior estate owner to pay taxes and interest on encumbrances.	5. Remainderman *cannot* compel estate owner to pay taxes or interest on encumbrances.

91. **(B)** A prospective purchaser of real estate or of an interest in real estate is chargeable with knowledge of what appears in the Grantor-Grantee Index, the legal record required to be maintained by the Recorder; generally, he is not chargeable with notice of that which appears in other records which may be kept as a convenience, such as a Tract Index. Thus, if Callahan prevails, it will be because the record of the mortgage in the Tract Index was outside this chain of title, and thus not constructive notice to third persons.

92. **(C)** An easement is deemed appurtenant when the right of special use benefits the holder of the easement in his physical use or enjoyment of another tract of land. For an easement appurtenant to exist, there must be two tracts of land. One is called the dominant tenement (which has the benefit of the easement). The second tract is the servient tenement (which is subject to the easement right). In the present case Oscar granted Groves an express easement to use the roadway as an access to Groves' adjacent property. Choice (A) is incorrect since a license is a revocable privilege to enter upon the lands of the licensor. Choice (B) is wrong

because an easement in gross is created where the holder of the easement interest acquires his right of special use in the servient tenement independently of his ownership or possession of another tract of land. Alternate (D) is erroneous since a prescriptive easement is not in writing, but arises through the long continued use of the property (as analogous to adverse possession).

93. **(A)** The provision in the 1950 agreement granted Groves an easement appurtenant that would "run with the land" and, thus, be enforceable against successors of the original parties. An easement appurtenant is, for purposes of succession, an incident of the possession of the dominant tenement. Even though an easement appurtenant is a property interest in the servient tenement rather than an interest in the dominant tenement, the easement privilege passes with the possession of the dominant tenement. As a consequence, the fact that Groves remained in possession of his adjacent dominant tenement is sufficient to establish his right to use the servient tenement in a manner consistent with the easement right.

94. **(D)** The covenants of seisin, right to convey, and against encumbrances are personal covenants which, from their nature, must be broken instantaneously on the delivery of the deed or they are never broken. It follows that such personal covenants never run with the land and, therefore, the subsequent grantee may not maintain a cause of action against the original grantor.

95. **(A)** Since the covenant against encumbrances (i.e., existence of mortgage) was breached at the instant of the delivery of the deed, Williams will succeed in his action because the encumbrance of the mortgage burdened the property at the time of conveyance, entitling him to recover the amount he was compelled to pay in principal and in interest with interest accruing from time of payment.

96. **(A)** First of all, note that the aforementioned recording act is a pure notice type statute. Under this type of statute the subsequent bona fide purchaser prevails over any prior interests whether the subsequent purchaser records or not. The subsequent purchaser's priority is determined by his status at the time he acquires his deed; there is no premium on his race to the recorder's office. Secondly, in referring to our factual situation, Oscar has a superior right in the property. At the time Oscar, purchased Scenicacre, Purchaser had not recorded. Consequently, Oscar, as a subsequent bona fide purchaser for value, had established his priority as soon as he purchased the property. Moreover, note that a subsequent bona fide purchaser in a notice jurisdiction is charged with notice of every recorded instrument of conveyance which is a link in his chain of title.

97. **(C)** The recording act referred to in this question is a ***race-notice type statute.*** Under such a statute, ***an unrecorded conveyance or other instrument is invalid as against a subsequent bona fide purchaser for value without notice who records "first."*** In effect, a race-notice statute combines the essential features of both the notice and race type recording statutes. In order for a subsequent party to prevail in a race-notice jurisdiction, he must be *both* a bona fide purchaser for value without notice of the prior interest *and* record first. In our hypothetical, Vendee was a subsequent BFP for value and without notice of the prior Ohner-to-Son deed. Moreover, Vendee purchased Scenicacre in 1975 and immediately recorded the deed. Vendee recorded his deed first in time. (Note: Oscar did not purchase the property

until 1979). Thus, Vendee is the record titleholder of Scenicacre in 1980 under this race-notice recording statute.

98. **(A)** In 1980, Oscar would succeed in an action to quiet title to Scenicacre under a race-notice type recording statute. To reiterate, the recording act in the previous question is a race-notice type statute. In order to gain priority of title in a race-notice jurisdiction, a subsequent party must be (1) a BFP for value without notice of any prior interests and (2) record first. Since Buyer and Vendee were both aware of the existence of the prior Ohner-to-Son deed, the notice requirement could not be met as to them. Furthermore, Purchaser, who was unaware of any prior interests, failed to record first in time. Therefore, Oscar would prevail since he was the only party to satisfy both requirements; he was a subsequent BFP for value without notice (paying $25,000 for the property) and was the first to record (between Purchaser and himself).

99. **(B)** Be advised in this example that the reciprocal rights of first refusal must "vest," if at all, during the respective lifetimes of Anderson and Barrington. As such, since Anderson is a measuring life, we will know within Anderson's lifetime whether he will exercise his option to purchase Barrington's land. Consequently, there is no violation of the rule.

Multistate Nuance Chart:

PROPERTY

RULE AGAINST PERPETUITIES AS APPLIED TO OPTIONS TO PURCHASE LAND

OPTIONS CONTAINED IN A DEED INSTRUMENT	OPTIONS CONTAINED IN A LEASEHOLD CONTRACT
R/P Applies	R/P Does Not Apply

100. **(B)** It is important to point out that in a joint tenancy each joint tenant owns the **whole of the property** and that he does **not** own a share or fractional part thereof. In this regard, a joint tenant may convey away his entire interest in jointly owned property or dispose of a fractional part thereof. Thus, in the present example Amy's deed to Cooke carved out and vested in Cooke an undivided one-half interest in the North East Quarter of Blackacre which Cooke owned as a tenant in common with Brooke. Next, since a joint tenant has the right and power voluntarily to dispose of his interest in jointly owned property, his creditors have the right and power to take that interest involuntarily. Therefore, Amy's judgment creditor, Drake, had the right to levy upon and sell Amy's interest in the South Half of Blackacre. As such, Brooke and Zorn are tenants in common of the South Half of Blackacre, each owning an undivided one-half interest therein. Finally, with respect to the North West Quarter of Blackacre, Amy and Brooke remained joint tenants of that Quarter until Amy's death. Brooke's right of survivorship defeats the right of Amy's surviving heir, Hilton. Consequently, Hilton can claim no interest in the North West Quarter of Blackacre.

MIG 1   FEDERAL JUDICIAL AUTHORITY

Fee Simple Absolute ───────── How created ─────→ A conveys Blackacre "to B and his heirs."

(Common law) ──────────────────────────────── words of limitation

FEE SIMPLE

Fee Simple Determinable
(created by words: "until,"
"while," "as long as")

A conveys Blackacre "to B and his heirs as long as liquor is not sold on property."

Exam Tip: If event occurs, there is an ***automatic reversion*** back to grantor.

Fee Simple Subject To Condition Subsequent
(created by words: "provided that," "but if,"
"on condition that").

A conveys Blackacre "to B and her heirs but if liquor is sold on property, then A has right of re-entry."

Fee Simple Subject To Executory Interest

A conveys "to B and her heirs but if liquor is sold on property then to C and his heirs."

Exam Tip: If event occurs, title passes to a 3rd person (***no*** reversion to grantor).

───── How created ───── A by deed conveys Blackacre "to B and the heirs of his body."

──────────────────────────────── words of limitation

FEE TAIL

Inheritance to a particular
group of lineal descendants

A conveys Blackacre "to B and the male heirs of his body."

───── How created ───── A by deed (or will) conveys Blackacre "to B for life."

Life Estate Pur Autre Vie ⌐ A by deed (or will) conveys Blackacre "to B for the life of C."

LIFE ESTATE

Dower

At common law a widow was entitled to a life estate in 1/3 of the land that her husband owned (seised) in fee simple during marriage.

Created by operation of law

Curtesy

At common law a husband was entitled (upon his wife's death) to a life estate in ***all*** lands his wife owned during the marriage.

multistate issue graph

MIG 2   NON-FREEHOLD ESTATES

ESTATE FOR YEARS

— How created —— L leases Blackacre to T for the period January 1, 1992 to December 31, 1994 (a period of 3 years).

Characteristics
- Specific time for beginning and ending
- Ends automatically
- Subject to statute of frauds

PERIODIC TENANCY also referred to as **ESTATE FROM YEAR TO YEAR**

— How created —— L leases Blackacre to T "from month to month" Characteristics (or year to year).

Characteristics
- No specific termination date
- Automatically renews
- Notice is required for termination

TENANCY AT WILL

— How created —— L leases Blackacre to T for "as long as L wishes."

Characteristics
- Either party may terminate at will.
- No notice is required.
- Terminates by operation of law:
  (1) either party dies;
  (2) tenant commits waste; or
  (3) landlord sells property.

TENANCY AT SUFFERANCE (Hold-over Tenant)

T **_wrongfully_** remains in possession of premises **_after_** the expiration of a lawful tenancy.

Landlord Remedies
- Eviction
- Creation of periodic tenancy
- Forcible entry, which most states by statute prohibit

KAPLAN) **pmbr**

multistate issue graph

MIG 3 FUTURE INTERESTS

REVERSION

How created — A, owner in fee simple, conveys Blackacre to B for life. (A has a reversion.)

Characteristics
- Is not destructible
- Is transferable
- Is vested
- Is *NOT* subject to rule against perpetuities

POSSIBILITY OF REVERTER

How created — A, owner in fee simple, conveys Blackacre to B and his heirs as long as property is used for residential purposes.

Characteristics
- Takes effect *automatically* upon happening of event
- Created as part of determinable fee
- Alienable

RIGHT OF RE-ENTRY FOR BROKEN CONDITION (Power of Termination)

How created — A, owner in fee simple, conveys Blackacre to B and his heirs but if land is not used for residential purposes, A has right of re-entry.

Characteristics
- Never takes effect automatically.
- Created as part fee simple subject to condition subsequent.
- Not subject to RAP.

REMAINDERS

Vested — A, owner in fee simple, conveys Blackacre to C and his heirs. (C has a vested remainder).

Not subject to RAP

Contingent — A, owner in fee, conveys Blackacre to B for life, remainder to C and his heirs if C pays A $100. (C has a contingent remainder).

TYPES
- Absolutely vested
- Vested subject to *partial defeasance*
- Vested subject to total defeasance
  - Must follow natural termination of prior estate
  - Follows a life estate, fee tail or estate for years
  - Cannot follow a fee simple estate
- Subject to condition precedent
- Created in favor of an unborn or unascertained person
  - Not destructible (modern view)
  - Are transferable (modern view)
  - Subject to claims of creditors (modern view)
  - Subject to RAP

TYPES

EXECUTORY INTERESTS

Shifting — A, owner in fee, conveys Blackacre to B for life, but if B marries C, then to C and his heirs. (C has a shifting executory interest).

Springing — A, owner in fee, devises Blackacre to B and his heirs one year after A's death. (B has a springing executory devise.)

Characteristics
- Cuts short prior estate before its natural termination
- Prior estate may be a fee simple, life estate or fee tail
- Subject to RAP
- Alienable and contingent

multistate issue graph

MIG 4   NON-POSSESSORY INTERESTS IN LAND

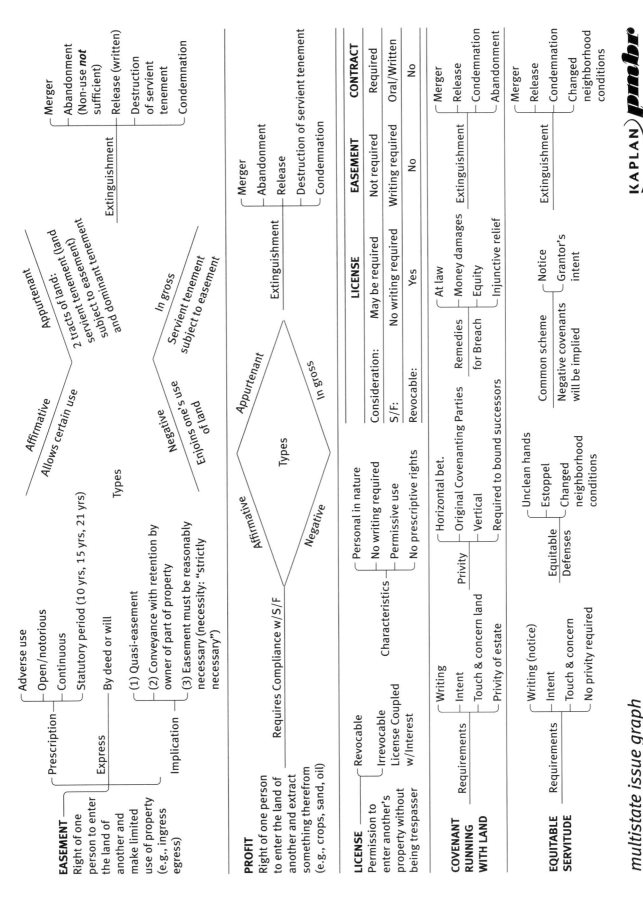

multistate issue graph

KAPLAN) *pmbr*

MIG 5 CONVEYANCING

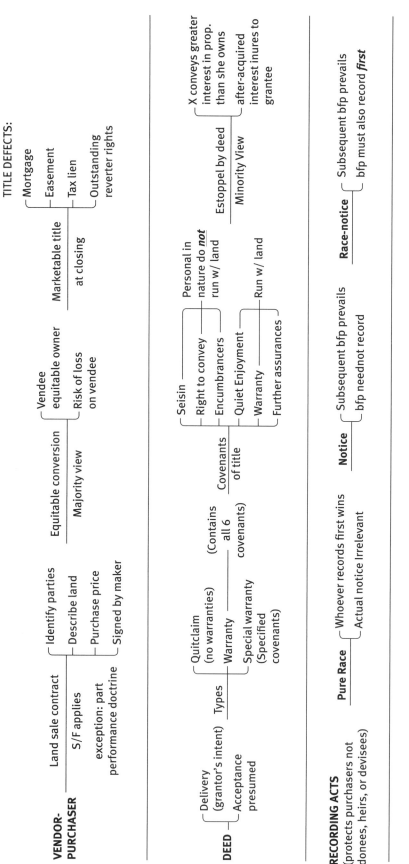

VENDOR-PURCHASER

- Land sale contract
  - S/F applies
    - exception: part performance doctrine
  - Identify parties
  - Describe land
  - Purchase price
  - Signed by maker
- Equitable conversion
  - Majority view
  - Vendee equitable owner
    - Risk of loss on vendee
- Marketable title
  - at closing
  - **TITLE DEFECTS:**
    - Mortgage
    - Easement
    - Tax lien
    - Outstanding reverter rights

DEED

- Delivery (grantor's intent)
- Acceptance presumed
- Types
  - Quitclaim (no warranties)
  - Warranty (Contains all 6 covenants)
  - Special warranty (Specified covenants)
- Covenants of title
  - Seisin
  - Right to convey
  - Encumbrancers
  - Quiet Enjoyment
  - Warranty
  - Further assurances
  - Personal in nature do **not** run w/ land
  - Run w/ land
- Estoppel by deed
  - Minority View
    - X conveys greater interest in prop. than she owns
    - after-acquired interest inures to grantee

RECORDING ACTS (protects purchasers not donees, heirs, or devisees)

- **Pure Race**
  - Whoever records first wins
  - Actual notice Irrelevant
- **Notice**
  - Subsequent bfp prevails
  - bfp neednot record
- **Race-notice**
  - Subsequent bfp prevails
  - bfp must also record **first**

MORTGAGES (Security interest in land)

- Types
  - Lien theory
  - Title theory
    - Transfer legal title to mortgagee
- **Redemption** (generally mortgagor has redemp rt.)
  - Equity: mortgagor can pay off mortgage prior to foreclosure
  - Statutory: mortgagor can redeem for some fixed period after foreclosure
- **PRIORITIES** (Determined by time when mortgage is recorded)
  - Prior mortgage prevails over subsq. one
  - Unrecorded mortgage not protected
  - Foreclosure proceeds insufficient deficiency judgment allowed
  - Transfer by mortgagor: grantee who assumes mortgage becomes personally liable.

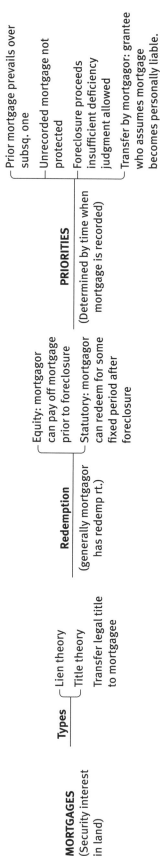

multistate issue graph

MIG 6   CONCURRENT ESTATES

TENANCY IN COMMON

Created — A conveys Blackacre "to C and D and their heirs, each taking a ½ interest."

Unity of Possession

Incidents of co-ownership
- No right of survivorship
- Co-tenant has right to possess all of property
- Co-tenant need not share profits
- Co-tenant has right to share rents

Duties
- No fiduciary relation between co-tenants
- Ouster allowed

JOINT TENANCY

Created at Common law — "to B and C and their heirs."

Modern view — "to B and C and their heirs as joint tenants."

4 Unities "TTIP"
- Time
- Title
- Interest
- Possession

Severance
- Conveyance inter vivos tenancy in common results
- Partition
- Mortgage (title theory)
- Death
- Right of Survivorship

SPECIAL SITUATIONS INVOLVING SEVERANCE BY CONVEYANCE

1. A-B-C own Blackacre as joint tenants. A conveys his interest to D. B-C own Blackacre as joint tenants and D as a tenant in common.

2. A-B own Blackacre as joint tenants. A conveys 30% of the property to C. A-B own 70% of Blackacre as joint tenants and B-C own 30% as tenants in common.

TENANCY BY THE ENTIRETY

Created — "to H and W, husband and wife, and their heirs."

5 Unities "TTIPP"
- Time
- Title
- Interest
- Possession
- Person

Severance
- Conveyance if both spouses join in
- Divorce
- Death
- Right of survivorship

multistate issue graph

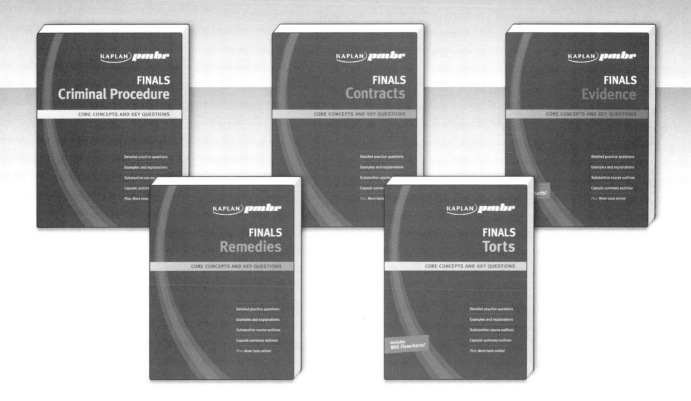

With products serving children, adults, schools and businesses, Kaplan has an educational solution for every phase of learning.

KIDS AND SCHOOLS

SCORE! Educational Centers offer individualized tutoring programs in reading, math, writing and other subjects for students ages 4-14 at more than 160 locations across the country. We help students achieve their academic potential while developing self-confidence and a love of learning.
www.escore.com

We also partner with schools and school districts through Kaplan K12 Learning Services to provide instructional programs that improve results and help all students achieve. We support educators with professional development, innovative technologies, and core and supplemental curriculum to meet state standards.
www.kaplank12.com

TEST PREP AND ADMISSIONS

Kaplan Test Prep and Admissions prepares students for more than 80 standardized tests, including entrance exams for secondary school, college and graduate school, as well as English language and professional licensing exams. We also offer private tutoring and one-on-one admissions guidance.
www.kaptest.com

HIGHER EDUCATION

Kaplan Higher Education offers postsecondary programs in fields such as business, criminal justice, health care, education, and information technology through more than 70 campuses in the U.S. and abroad, as well as online programs through Kaplan University and Concord Law School.
www.khec.com • *www.kaplan.edu* • *www.concordlawschool.edu*

PROFESSIONAL

If you are looking to start a new career or advance in your field, Kaplan Professional offers training to obtain and maintain professional licenses and designations in the accounting, financial services, real estate and technology industries. We also work with businesses to develop solutions to satisfy regulatory mandates for tracking and compliance.
www.kaplanprofessional.com

Kaplan helps individuals achieve their educational and career goals.
We build futures one success story at a time.